Management Vitality

The Team Approach

Donald A. Spartz
Author

Judy D. Stranahan
Editor

Published by
Society of Manufacturing Engineers
Publications/Marketing Services Division
One SME Drive • P.O. Box 930
Dearborn, Michigan 48121

Management Vitality: A Team Approach

© 1984
Society of Manufacturing Engineers
Dearborn, Michigan 48121

First Edition
First Printing

Manufactured in the United States of America

Library of Congress Catalog Card Number: 84-050172

International Standard Book Number: 0-87263-143-5

Table of Contents

ACKNOWLEDGEMENTS

My friend and associate, Rosemarie S. Pishnery, is credited with reading drafts, and constantly prodding me to rewrite the text. Rosemarie supervised the typing of these countless drafts, and interpreted my atrocious handwriting through the entire process. She deserves my warmest thanks.

My longtime friend, Roman F. Diekemper, reviewed, criticized, offered suggestions, and gave advice. My special thanks to Roman for Chapter 10, which after some prodding, he volunteered to write. Roman was able to relate to the other chapters and their impact on quality, service, commitment and excellence.

My friend and brother, John, reviewed an early crude draft and at this key developmental stage, offered me encouragement and challenge to continue with the work. His continued support in reviewing the final draft was of great assistance.

Robert Gifford, a client, reviewed a final draft, which he felt was sound and would be required reading for every supervisor-manager and student of management.

Russell S. Pishnery, a Journalism-Communication student who had never been exposed to an industrial environment, read an early draft of the text, disagreed with some parts, and didn't understand other sections. I then knew that I was on the right course.

Our clients, who have a right to privacy and cannot be mentioned by name, are the people I owe the most to in the development of this book. It is the experience I gained in working with them that made this book possible.

A special thanks to my mother Bertha, who can best be described as a beautiful lady. Her patience and understanding along with my father John's integrity, provided sound, inherent values.

A special thanks to Judy Stranahan of SME for her professional editing of the final text.

PREFACE

After 22 years of working with managers, the most frequently asked question is still, "Where can I obtain a book on the revitalization of management?" There is no single academic volume which I can recommend which is practical, effective, and at the same time, hard-hitting and to the point.

Why is this so? Possibly because many of our learning institutions are trying to explain behavior, while industry and society are trying to control without understanding behavior. Neither activity by itself, will achieve success.

The elements and subjects necessary to put the role of the manager of the '80s into perspective in the development of people and improvement in productivity, are contained in this book. The term "manager" includes all managers from first line supervision through top levels of management. This is a "how-to" book. Management theory, while not ignored, is essentially being left in the institutions of higher learning.

Our American management system has become entrenched with traditional management techniques, many of which are outdated. This has resulted in practices that have fostered stagnation and produced status quo and survival managers who lack the ability and qualifications to provide the basic sound leadership necessary to bring about change. These are the major contributing factors for the declining productivity in this country.

Productivity is declining because the work force is "turned off" and resistant to techniques used by traditional managers. Negative, nonproductive attitudes in the work force are created and reinforced by managers who are not prepared and not qualified to lead and to assist employees.

The attitudes and resistance created by outmoded management practices have crippled the communication process that is essential in any organization. Too frequently, the direction of communication is one-way from top to bottom, with no time or need to listen to the employee.

Some would have us believe that we can motivate employees with gimmicks, material rewards, and job enrichment, all of which have failed.

These techniques have been used as a substitute for good sound management principles and practices.

Discipline in management and in the work force is often sporadic and inconsistent. One extreme is that management no longer runs the company. Another extreme is rigid, unbending control which retards initiative, motivation, creativity and growth. The extremes have evolved from the traditional top-down communication management of do as I dictate, to a philosophy that the labor force runs the firm. Both extremes result in an on-going adverse labor-management environment.

Useful objective performance evaluations which are the tools of sound management, are almost nonexistent. There are numerous checklists of traits which have little or nothing to do with job performance. The like/dislike factors are evident and the evaluation is guided by personal feelings or opinion. The criteria for evaluations are often taken from lengthy job descriptions which sound impressive but fail to include how well an individual must perform, the results that are desired, or the standards of performance expected.

Supervisors are often selected from the work force based on work performance and job skills. These are usually unrelated to the requirements and responsibilities of supervision. The training of a new supervisor-manager is too often by trial and error, nonexistent, or by an individual who is in training and ill prepared to effectively deal with or understand the management system and the organizational culture. A promotion often means "arrival", i.e., just maintain status quo and continue doing what the predecessor did for years. Not knowing or realizing that what we did yesterday was not necessarily correct then or effective today.

Organizations often operate internally like several separate companies or entities. Productivity is low because the various leadership and management styles are not understood. This leads to unresolved conflict, is the underlying cause of poor attitudes, and certain practices then become suppressed. The identification and resolution of conflicts and problems are opportunities for improvement of productivity. This requires an openness to change, mixed with creative imagination.

The current emphasis on improving productivity has caused managers to become more aware of their responsibilities and the limitations in relying solely on continued improvement through technological advances. There is an increasing recognition that tremendous productivity gains can be achieved by improving the skills of the workers, supervisors, and managers. In addition, the cost/benefit of improving these skills is impressive in comparison with many of the technological capital improvements. However, technological advances and improvements must be pursued. The development of people all too often considered a luxury, cannot be ignored. There must be a balance between the two with equal emphasis. Without skilled workers, skilled supervisors, and effective participatory team management practices, the technological improvements will not be fully utilized and the true potential in productivity will not be achieved.

People, not capital spending, are the key to quality, service and productivity. Capital expenditure on equipment and automation will never be fully utilized until individual potential is developed and a sound organizational culture exists. More time and energy is spent researching, engineering, developing and/or making decisions on purchasing of capital equipment than is spent on developing people.

About ten years ago, I was on the telephone calling key executives for an appointment to present my services. This is not an easy task, since executives are continually bombarded with telephone calls and literature. A president and owner who was an exception to the norm, temporarily challenged my self-confidence. After introducing myself, the company, our services, and requesting an appointment, his response was: "Listen, I've been managing this company for twenty-five years. I don't need an ____ ____ like you".

His response and attitude were understandable. Many managers have been "burned" by experts professing to have all the answers, advocating gimmicks, and promising more than they are capable of delivering. This manager needed help. However, due to past experiences, his mind was closed. Two years later his company was bankrupt and out of business.

It is interesting to note that almost without exception, every organization we have worked with was successful prior to our development programs. Common with all was the recognized need to improve if they as managers, and as an organization, were to enjoy continued success through growth and profits. Sound leadership with a commitment to total development was present in these organizations. These are the same organizations that concentrate on goals and long-term plans vs. short-term activities and quarterly results.

There are proven methods of improving productivity, growth and profits through people. My objective in writing this book is to provide sufficient guidelines for some of the essential elements in improving productivity through revitalization and development. In doing so, I hope to challenge the reader and provide stimulation in a positive and constructive manner with practical proven answers.

I strongly believe and suggest that problems, barriers and conflicts in developing effective managers and improving productivity need to be confronted and resolved. My intention in writing has been to identify some of these problems, barriers and conflicts. Once they are identified and analyzed, a manager can intelligently develop goals and plans for change. I have attempted to avoid compromising and smoothing over to please all. As a result, certain statements may upset some readers. The degree of conflict will be determined by the differences in our beliefs, experiences and objectives.

American management practices must be revitalized before we can improve productivity and creativity. Our American financial management system requires disclosure of the financial condition every three months and to exhibit progress every quarter. As a result, managers are often under the influence of shortsighted management.

Top management must lead, develop commitments, and seek and support positive changes. The emphasis today is on crisis management, a technique much like fire fighting. Middle management, often the internal barriers, using traditional-autocratic management practices, must change from control and suppression to openness and candor. First line supervision must change from expeditors and enforcers, to advisors, assistants and teachers. While top management is involved with both short and long-term planning, the first line supervisor must be concerned with the day-to-day activities and short-term planning. The workers must be brought into the system through participation with a commitment to excellence.

This book includes findings from our studies, teachings, and experiences, and represents some of our beliefs in revitalization and development of an organization. The problems we have presented with the concepts and principles are essentially the same in all industries. Productivity problems exist throughout an organization in the blue and white-collar ranks.

We have attempted to point out weaknesses and managerial failures and what changes need to take place if managers are to revitalize management practices and improve productivity through the development of a sound organizational culture.

This productivity resource development book was designed to challenge each manager and provide guidelines for change. The reader's goal should be to seek the best solution. We encourage the reader to objectively assess present practices, identify opportunities for change, and start the process to revitalize the organization through development.

Examples of companies in this book are taken from published, accessible sources and from personal contacts. In the Developmental Case

Studies found in the *Appendix*, the names of companies and people do not reflect their real names. Sufficient changes were made as to company identification. The reader can be assured that where a manufacturer is mentioned, the firm is not a manufacturer. When a firm is mentioned as being in the southwest, it is in fact, located elsewhere. The facts illustrated are accurate, the specific companies involved have been carefully disguised.

The terms supervisor-manager-boss-superior are intended to be descriptive in a specific situation. The terms are intended to have the same meaning. The term he/his is used rather than constantly repeating he/she or his/her.

Don Sparts

1

MANAGEMENT PERSPECTIVES

While conducting a workshop on productivity, 30 corporate executives and plant managers were asked to define the term "productivity". One of the individuals indicated that everyone knows the meaning of productivity. However, when asked for a definition of the term, there was a period of silence. Each individual was then asked to put in writing their definition of the term "productivity", and also how they measure productivity in their organization.

Their facial expression told the story. Out of the entire group, only four partially defined the term close to what is generally given as the standard definition. When it came to measurement, it was even more revealing. Very few measured productivity. They just instinctively "knew" when their units were productive. Most indicated that the bottom line figures told them whether they were productive.

I suggested that waiting to measure until the bottom line figures are received, may be too late. The bottom line for a manager may mean goals were met in production numbers, while for a CEO, it may mean production was at a loss. Does the bottom line really measure productivity? The temptation to fix short-term figures to please the investors and Wall Street analysts may lead to long-term disaster. The bottom line figure is a measurement of history.

Effective managers measure productivity on a daily basis. In many organizations, a computer printout detailing exactly what was produced daily by each machine line, is available by 9:00 the next morning. The printout reflects pounds/units, the manhours per unit, the amount shipped, including all other charges, and is converted into dollars with the profit or loss for the day. On the same single computer printout, there is data for the month to date and year to date, with a comparison of the previous periods. That is short-term monitoring of results. The 5-10-15 year long plans based on goals are equally necessary.

Productivity has been defined as: The ratio of output to inputs...the relationship between the amount of goods and services produced and the quantity and quality of human, capital and natural resources needed to produce them. Productivity is the output of capital resources, natural resources and human resources.

The control of these three elements is established by people...people comprising various levels of management including engineers, accountants, technicians and the workers. Human resources, people guided by a dominate leadership and management style is that element which determines all other elements, i.e., the type of labor, staff personnel, capital expenditures, the utilization of natural resources and the product mix, all of which determines productivity. The level of productivity is determined by human knowledge, skills, attitude and behavior. When these factors are not sound, problems in quality, schedules, service and overall productivity prevail.

Since human resources determine productivity, we will concentrate on how a manager can develop, lead and direct human resources, and provide motivation to improve productivity through Participative Team Management concepts and practices. In Participative Team Management, communications on all levels is emphasized, especially listening and acting on ideas and suggestions from all members of the team. Directing human resources is not a function of the Human Resource Department, but a function of every manager on a daily basis.

One of our most serious problems today is that managers have become complacent. They accept the status quo. Executive Pete Estes of General Motors stated, "When something has been done a particular way for 15 or 20 years, it is a pretty good sign, in these changing times, that it is being done the wrong way". He has since altered this statement by changing "15 or 20" to five. With the present status of the automobile industry, it probably should be changed from five to one.

In management development programs, managers are told that if they are doing their jobs today the same way they did them one year ago, they are not growing; they are on their way to stagnation. More specifically, they are "caretakers", having resigned themselves to status quo. They have ceased to learn and grow. They operate with no imagination. An individual producing no more today than one year ago, has reduced the profit margin since cost has risen with no additional output. As a result, productivity declines.

There are many factors, controlled by management, which contribute to or create declining productivity. Because these factors are controllable, the drop in productivity must be viewed as a failure of the management system.

In every organization there is an identifiable management system and organizational culture. Organizational culture being defined as: "The combined management styles, practices and beliefs which determine the level of activities, the degree of motivation, creativity, and the working environment".

Although each organization has a system and culture, there is little uniformity from one organization to another. Each organization's system and culture is reflective of the beliefs and management style of the senior management personnel. Each individual's management practices or style is based on their beliefs, experiences, training, the organization's policies, and the procedures within the organization. There are normally several different systems or unsound management styles which, unless recognized for their impact and changed, result in unresolved conflicts and a suppression or disguise of problems.

The Traditional Autocrat

There are wide variations in management styles from one organization to another. At the extreme and possibly the most prominent, is the traditional autocrat who preaches, "I am the boss, I know what needs to be done, and I know how to do it and get results". In the next breath the autocrat will, in frustration, explain that the problem is the employees.

The autocrat blames the employees because he believes they don't want to work, they are lazy, will not accept responsibility, are not productive, and are only interested in putting in their eight hours and going home. This managerial style creates negative attitudes and negative expectations which produce negative results. The subordinate's reactions merely reinforce the autocrat's "belief" that workers are not what they used to be and must be disciplined, controlled, and closely supervised.

The wide range of differences between managers in their individual managerial style is quite apparent. Some make the choice to listen, others choose to "lean-on" or pressure employees without effectively communicating. Many managers make a deliberate effort to truly communicate, while others exhibit authority. Visible differences appear when managers are genuinely interested in obtaining employees' ideas for change, while others are suppressing the employees and their ideas.

The autocrat is preoccupied in protecting and putting defenses around his position of authority. His behavior is always defending his actions. He is seen by subordinates as a weak form of management. As a result, a lack of

3

trust and respect develops. If any relationship is to be effective, there must be complete trust and respect. The autocrat prefers to see himself as strong, while subordinates see him as he really is, which in simplest terms means he is viewed as being weak and insecure.

Autocratic managing is management by manipulation. My will, want, wish, and whim will be done, is the autocrat's theme. Witness this in his meeting with the workers. They are told what is wrong with their work attitudes, what is wrong with their work habits and what is wrong with them as individuals. How can such employees have the gall to question the actions of their superior, considering all he had done for them? How could they step out of place, by offering suggestions on how to improve productivity?

The Progressive Manager

By comparison, there are many other managers who are highly effective and humanly sensitive to developing open communications and employee feedback. The goal of these progressive and sensitive managers is to process and act on information and ideas, not to protect the status quo by making excuses. They are managers who seek the sustaining and binding interplay of contact and concern, rather than constriction and control. Effective managers want not only to listen, but also to hear. They are managers who recognize that people, being human like themselves, have a sincere interest in being involved in creative thinking, problem identification and problem solving. Such managers also recognize that at all times there is probably someone in the work force who is more knowledgable than he, who is closer to the problem, and has the skill to act on a potential opportunity.

Problems and conflicts are actually opportunities for managers to improve productivity. The progressive manager recognizes that his employees are each an extension of himself and will multiply his effectiveness with sound leadership.

There are marked differences between managers in the ways they obtain and handle employee feedback. The differences in their assumptions and attitudes about their employees and their wide diversity in management styles, account for the difference in employee job commitment. Douglas McGregor[1] found in his research that managerial attitudes and assumptions of employees produced a definite impact on:

1. Job identification.
2. Waste and manufacturing scrap rates.
3. Number and intensity of employee grievances.
4. Level of productivity.

5. Absenteeism and tardiness.

6. Employee turnover.

In those departments and work areas where the managers had an involved participative and assisting relationship with employees, employee motivation and productivity were above average. In those departments with autocratic managers, there was below average motivation, higher turnover and grievance rates, and ineffective adversarial relationships between management and labor.

Many years have passed since Douglas McGregor published his findings. Unfortunately, we have not learned or have not been honest with ourselves, have not faced up to or recognized the negative impact certain management leadership styles have on employees, on productivity, and on the organization's future.

Why do some managers choose to project themselves through Participative Team Managing, while other "leaders" continue demanding that followers work based on fear and domination? What underlies those behaviors which seek to produce inferior feelings in others or at the very least, feelings that they are an insignificant part of the system?

Our attitudes and beliefs determine our behavior which tells people what we are. We are what we believe about ourselves and others. The domineering and dogmatic leader sees danger, threat, or potential harm. He believes employees will take advantage, therefore, he must stay alert and be in charge..."employees are basically lazy"..."stay on top of them or they will goof-off". The best defense is an aggressive offense even if it means being offensive. Winning is everything. These are the trademarks of the autocratic manager. He also blasts and belittles other managers at staff meetings. His belief that others are concerned only for themselves and that their concern for the organization is nil. What he doesn't recognize is that he has created an organizational culture which retards an organization, lowers productivity and limits creativity. He fails to perceive that the most effective management tool, is people to people management, or Participative Team Managing.

A manager in the automotive industry recently attempted to dispel the fact it might be management's fault that it lost $631 million in one year. The problem he explains is the lazy workers who don't show up for work. "We've got the same technology as Japan. We've got the same engineering. We can build the same cars as Japan if we can just get a day's work for a day's pay".

The traditional autocratic management style that has for years been accepted almost without question, is now being recognized as destructive. After all, is it really practical and honest to blame employees for the decline in productivity? Are not employees attitudes and behavior reflective of management's? The attitudes, commitment or lack of commitment of employees are in fact created by the actions of management.

Dr. Blake and Dr. Mouton in their book, *The New Managerial Grid,*[2] define and produce an in-depth discussion of the five most prominent management styles and the impact on an organization. Blake and Mouton describe the five styles as authority-obedience, country club manager, improvished manager, the organization man, and the team manager. Their work in this area is sound.

The Organizational Culture

We can learn from Japan's management system and the impact it has on productivity. There, supervisors and managers are considered teachers, assistants and advisors to the workers. The worker's ideas and suggestions are encouraged and incorporated into the job. On a new job, the worker is asked how the job might best be done. In Japan, worker participation and involvement developed because of their organizational culture. The organizational culture in Japan is entirely different than the organizational culture in America.

Overnight experts attempting to lift certain elements and piecemeal the Japanese quality circle approach into our present management systems, are failing. They are failing because our organizational culture is not the same as Japan's. Organizations that do have a sound culture already have worker-manager participation. Organizations successfully using quality circles had a sound organizational culture prior to the QC program.

High productivity is achieved by the organizational culture being sound with all elements working together as a single unit. In Japan, quality circles are a single element in their culture, which is conducive to listening and obtaining worker participation and involvement. In this country, we are still learning how to listen, achieve participation and involvement, and develop a nonadversarial working relationship.

The management system of an organization is determined by the dominant leadership and management styles. It can be a system of supervision and rigid control with the use of authority, or one of openness and participation with a motivated workforce seeking the best results through teamwork.

The opportunities and the need to improve our management effectiveness have never been greater. We are entering a period which requires that the entire system be revitalized. To be revitalized means that change must take place. In order for change to take place, individuals must see the need to change. They must know that change is encouraged, solicited and accepted. Change is resisted where there is a lack of trust, respect, and sound leadership.

The task of changing and becoming more effective is a challenge that requires an organized systematic approach. Change requires that one recognize where he is today, where he wants to be tomorrow, and then establish the goals to bring about change. Effective managers recognize that they must continue to learn and grow or become obsolete. The individual that knows it all has ceased to learn and grow. As a consequence, his leadership is no longer sound.

Individual and organizational growth is not a short-term or sporadic process. Effective change requires an organized and systematic plan with specific goals and measurable activities and results. Change in management needs to be based on sound proven behavioral principles.

Our problems in managing have developed for a multitude of reasons. One reason is how management has been defined in the past. The simplistic definition given to describe what management does has been: "Management gets things done through other people". Many have taken this literally and have gotten things done through people in an autocratic manner with a total disregard for people as human beings, and thus the resultant long-term damage. In our society today, this is no longer acceptable as sound management. People/employees at all levels need to feel a part of an organization—trusted, respected, and recognized as equals. To recognize and accept the need to change is difficult for the autocratic manager. He thinks that others must change, according to his direction.

There is a high degree of self deception in each of us and our perceived management style. The fact is supported by comparisons of management style surveys completed by managers and their subordinates. Frequently, the surveys completed by subordinates are quite different from the way managers have perceived themselves to be.

The task is to develop a sound organizational culture. A culture consisting of trust, open and candid communications, effective listening, and participation. A culture with management and leadership styles, practices and actions which encourage creativity and growth through Participative Team Management concepts.

Individuals must want to change or no change will take place. No one individual or organization can develop someone who does not want to develop or grow. Creating the desire to change requires effective sound leadership.

1. Douglas McGregor, *The Human Side of Enterprise* (New York: McGraw-Hill, 1958).
2. Robert R. Blake and Jane S. Mouton, *The New Managerial Grid* (Houston, Texas: Gulf Publishing Company, 1978), pp. 16-155.

2

THE CHANGING WORKER

The change in the attitudes and values toward work and the quality of the personal life of young people and others in the present work force has been dramatic. The eight-hour job with reasonable security is no longer good enough. Individuals want and need job satisfaction, a sense of achievement, recognition, and treatment as human beings. For sometime there has been an awareness that people are changing, rejecting leadership, resisting authority and in general, rejecting the work ethic that made America the industrial leader of the past. The gradual change of the last 20 years has not been fully understood or has management learned how to universally cope with it. Workers are more educated and more sophisticated, and management will need to change accordingly.

Young people in a post-industrial society are no longer attracted by industry to work in a plant. In addition, many are not taught what they need to know in school or in the home to effectively work as production workers in plants. Many youngsters do not have to work as they are growing up due to the fact that Mom and Dad can always provide. Consequently, these people are not psychologically prepared for certain types of work, especially as laborers, in entry level and semiskilled jobs. As a way of life, such jobs are considered unacceptable. It should be noted that in a recession such as the '82-'83 economic decline, work of any kind becomes more attractive. This will change as the economy improves.

To most young people, plant/manufacturing work is a four letter word. They want to start out with all of the conveniences they enjoyed in the home of their parents. This is impossible to do on a starting wage. These people frequently don't think of long-term growth and don't aspire to a corporate career. They believe they should be able to immediately acquire a job as good as Dad's.

Frequently, business and economic courses are poorly taught in school and in many cases, the only job many instructors have ever experienced was instructing, working in research or governmental agencies, and consequently, have little understanding of how business earns money, where the money comes from and where it is spent.

Michael R. Sandercock a second year graduate student at Kent State University in a personal letter writes, "Your article on 'Developing an Organization That Listens', was very interesting. Every time I asked about Participative Management in my undergraduate classes, I was told to wait until I'm in graduate school. There is a definite need to educate future business persons on attitudes toward others on all levels of organizations. I think universities should ingrain these ideas right from the start of the program."[1] Mike is still waiting for a discussion on Participative Management.

Students often hear that businessmen exploit the workers, are spoiling the environment, care nothing about human values, and are "killing and maiming" workers to make a dollar. Profit has become a dirty word. Management is not to be trusted. Some of the attitudes of the demonstrators and activist of the '60s are a part of our educational system today.

Dr. Lawrence J. Peter in his, "Peter's Teacher—Education Theory" offers his explanation. "Those that can, do. Those that can't do, teach. Those that can't teach, teach the teachers. Those that can't teach the teachers get government grants."[2]

Factory jobs have negative images in the minds of young people. They find jobs in service industries such as the airlines, bars and hotels, more interesting. Which jobs are characterized in television? Usually not those in a factory. An interesting exception was Archie Bunker who quit his dull factory job as a shipping clerk to become part owner of a bar with a more glamorous life style. The productivity problems also exist in the so-called glamour industries, service industries, and other white collar jobs.

As a result of this conditioning, young people turn away from entry level and hard work jobs as a meaningful way of making a living. Those who are able to find work in the so-called glamour industries are considered to be the lucky ones. The "losers" are those who must work in a factory or an entry level office job. These are the very people who are not prepared for work and are not accustomed or prepared to be on time for work.

In spite of this, the young worker is smarter, and learns faster once he is motivated. The young worker is also impatient. Some have defensive "chips on their shoulders", distrust a company's motives, and are ready to rebel against typical restraints and disciplines, such as being on time and following

10

basic work rules. The young workers coming into the workplace with preformed attitudes due to education and experiences are not prepared for hard, sometimes dirty work, whether routine or complex. Quite often, the first day on the job, unqualified and/or insensitive management actions reinforces some of their negative feelings about a job.

A 1982 survey report by the Opinion Research Corporation said "white-collar, middle-management disenchanted with its superiors now has joined the more widely known white collar blues".[3] Other relevant findings in the survey demonstrate that workers miss the sense of accomplishment that once made their company a good place to work. Fifty percent of the workers say lack of corporate communications with the organization is a 'root cause' of sagging morale and declining productivity. Seventy percent believe management has lost touch with the rank and file worker and nearly 75% of lower echelon workers see little correlation between job performance and economic reward, and 53% believe they see inequities in compensation. William Schieman of Opinion Research said: "They now question one of the most basic assumptions, that the harder and better you work, the faster you'll get ahead". These attitudes are acquired from education, experiences and the way people are treated.

Our culture, home life and schools, do not prepare high school graduates to be solvent in personal financial management. To the contrary, through radio, television, billboards, and parental example, they are taught to buy now, enjoy, and pay later. Far too often the result is financial problems. Inability to pay bills and be solvent makes for a mentally concerned and aggravated worker. This results in poor concentration, a lack of positive thinking and tardiness. People with financial difficulties frequently extend that problem into their work and are not aware they are doing so.

The Basic Skills

Unless taught at home, many individuals lack the basic fundamental skills necessary to function in our culture. There is alarming evidence that a percentage of high school graduates cannot read or write and have difficulty with simple arithmetic. It has been estimated that 20% of the adults in the United States are functionally illiterate and another 30% are managing at what is regarded as only a marginal level. A second estimate is that 23 million people in the United States cannot adequately read or write. Some 43 million people barely read well enough to get along. These people are often the very workers we expect to read orders, quality specifications, and be promoted based on seniority.

A good percentage of our work force cannot speak, read or write the English language. Many companies have offered free classes in English, only to find no interest. Programs have been offered and canceled due to low attendance. The answer is when hiring, to make continued employment contingent upon the individual learning English within a reasonable time frame, or be terminated.

Educational experts are asking why many of our people lack these basic fundamental skills. Probably one of the answers is that many educators do not understand how to educate. Many teachers believe that because they have lectured for one hour, the students have learned.

The students and workers do not learn until they can actually apply their knowledge and acquire these skills. This means performing the actual mechanics necessary to acquire these skills. It means writing to acquire writing skills. Reading to acquire the skill of reading and understanding what has been printed. One cannot learn from experiences he has never had.

What does all of this have to do with improving productivity? It means the development of productive workers should start in the home, in the schools, and continue on the job. Courses must be meaningful and reflect realistic management concepts and practices. Basic courses should reflect the basic skills needed to perform basic tasks whether in the home or in the plant. It also means that our management system should recognize these problems and revitalize the system to develop people to ensure they possess the basic skills.

Because of the failure of the educational system to properly and realistically prepare individuals for work, the new worker walks into the employment office with a feeling of rejection, a feeling of failure, a conviction of being a second-class citizen. The individual applies for a job and is interviewed by an individual who quite often treats him as a second-class citizen. The applicant is not always viewed as a resource, but rather in some cases, as a potential problem needing control. The interviewer often conveys the feeling that he is doing the applicant a favor. Consequently, the applicant must express gratitude to feed the ego of the interviewer and increase his chances of being hired.

The interviewer frequently does not extend the courtesy of informing the applicant that he was not hired and why. This contributes to a negative attitude toward corporate management and promotes a negative perception of how a company treats their employees. Thus, a corporation's image is developed.

The decision to hire a certain individual is often made by someone other than the new employee's immediate superior. The worker needs a job and accepts it, not knowing where he or she will be working, the conditions that exist, or who his or her superior will be. Turnover is often high due to these factors. The superior was not involved in the selection process, therefore may feel no commitment to develop this new employee into a productive worker. Failure can be blamed on the hiring policy.

Orientation of the new employee usually consists of a review of the rules and regulations, restraints and controls, and the company benefits. The new worker is then told to report for work at the beginning of the next shift. The negative beliefs which this individual had toward management prior to applying have now been reinforced and confirmed by this process. Solidly negative attitudes have been formed. There is no commitment other than to obtain a job and get beyond the probationary period and have the security that is needed. The times and the opportunity for developing sound attitudes has passed.

The orientation presentations must be immediately done by the most qualified and enthusiastic people on a timely basis. The new employees must be given the whole picture of the firm, with enthusiasm and a positive attitude. He must be made to feel a necessary part of the firm, with quality and high performance being appreciated and recognized. Frequently, orientation consists of a canned audiovisual program which by itself is ineffective. The new employee needs to see leadership. This probably means eliminating the Training Department and having the orientation conducted by a leader—the new employee's immediate new supervisor—with an appearance and intro- duction by senior management. It is an opportunity to make the new employee feel necessary, important, and develop a commitment to quality and overall job performance.

Selecting the Worker

The first step in the process is to find potential workers within an area who may be interested in work in your type of operation. Participating in career days at local high schools along with a plant open house and a tour would be a start. A general file should be maintained to reflect open houses, employee referrals, former employees, and a list of qualified candidates who previously declined a job. Those who have the interest and have a reasonable chance of coping with the type of work that is available, can then be profiled to enable a zeroing in on the labor market.

Once these people are pinpointed, they need to be attracted to the company, and talked with individually about their possible future. They need to be told about the company's business and it should be explained that the job is a honorable, interesting, challenging, and rewarding position. The interest and need to stay with the company must be created if a commitment is to be developed. Consideration of an applicant's effectiveness and contribution should be given the same consideration as a major capital expenditure.

As part of the selection process, the applicant should see the job that is to be performed. The immediate manager or supervisor should make the final selection. Managers and/or supervisors can make or break a new employee due to personal likes and dislikes of the individual. The like/dislike factors may involve race, sex, appearance, or just the human chemistry between two people.

Once a new applicant is interested in working with your company, you have a chance to train them with proper job instructions. The young worker has the capabilities to learn fast if the superior is qualified to train, supervise, and convey a sense of responsibility, and is capable of truly delegating and obtaining a commitment from the individual. This sounds like a big order, however, it is the very minimum.

Minorities are often overlooked and excluded by employers because of employer's attitudes about their ability to learn and their desire to work. These attitudes must be identified and modified to reflect an openness with fair treatment. The attitudes of the potential employees must also be identified and understood. Once the attitudes are defined and we understand what the individual believes and why, then through communication, attitudes of the employee and employer can be changed. There is no room for individual prejudicies in management in an organization. The individuals who have personal prejudices which influence how they treat employees are not affordable. Once obstructions are removed, minority workers become productive and committed workers.

A sound selection, placement and development philosophy recognizes the basic need to be needed and to be recognized as human beings. People want to be responsible and effective when they are treated fairly and where they can see that their work serves a meaningful purpose.

Training the Worker

Typically, the new employee reports to the boss at the beginning of the work shift. This is the time when the manager is busy getting the shift started. They have a choice, to have the new employee sit and wait, or have a senior technically skilled person do the training. Again, the technically skilled person usually has no background or training skills necessary to train others.

Would it be so difficult for our Human Resource Department to have the new employee report to his supervisor in the middle of the shift on his first day of work?

Depending on the complexity of the job, very little training or shall we say proper training is provided the new employee. In addition, the senior person and the supervisor-manager have usually not been instructed as to the proper techniques and principles of job instruction. As a result, work is assigned with poor and incomplete instructions, resulting in the employee not knowing what the responsibilities are, how he is to perform or how his performance is to be evaluated. Workers who start with little respect for the employer and themselves, have confirmed their suspicions based on the way they have been treated. They will be distrustful of management and the organization. They will prod along and put in their eight hours.

Such management practices cause the workforce to resist productivity and innovative changes. The amount of work to be done will then require the consumption of the available time to do it. Change will be resisted until sound leadership is developed. The authoritarian manager in response to this will state: "There are those whose only goal in life is doing as little as they possibly can". He also communicates this attitude and as a result, his actions and expectations often come through.

The first line supervisor is often managing with autocratic practices and with fear techniques. This approach produces resistance, which forces the supervisor to take disciplinary measures. A commitment to quality, goals, and objectives is absent.

When line supervisors were asked in our surveys how they train new employees, 95% of the responses indicated that they did not know how to train. Out of thousands of supervisors, the response was much the same; we show him the job, tell him what to do, then turn him loose, sink or swim. Others sent the new employee to an experienced person for training where the employee received the same treatment. In each case, someone is saying let's put him to work and see if he can prove himself. When this takes place, we are in fact destroying instead of offering encouragement.

The following is a typical scenario as originally presented by James L. Hayes, of the American Management Association at a Management Development Conference held at the University of Wisconsin in 1969. (This same situation applies in white collar work, just change the job titles and the task.)

Frank is in charge of assembly. He desperately needs a drill press operator. He tells Sam, his superintendent, "Sam, I need a drill press operator and I would like to hire my brother-in-law, he's out of work and living in my house". Sam's reply is, "No, you can't do that, you know we have this EEOC program and the Human Resource Department has a minority applicant in the office that we must hire". Frank's personal prejudices and biases are in control. Sam says, "Sorry you must take him, we have no choice".

Robert, the new minority employee, is now asked by Frank if he knows how to operate a drill press. Robert states as most new employees do whether he can or not, that yes of course he can. Frank shows him the drill press and tells him that he is to take the parts out of a container on the left and drill a hole in the center of the part and then put the part in the container on the right. Frank then asks Robert if he understands and he, of course, indicates that he does. Frank then tells him to go ahead and do the job and if he has any questions he should call him.

At the end of the day, Robert has produced 100% scrap and rejects. Frank can now tell his superior, "See, I told you so, those guys are lazy, can't learn, don't do good work". Robert is terminated.

Frank then is allowed to hire his brother-in-law. He tells him what the job consists of by saying, "Take the parts, one at a time, out of the container on the left, inspect it, make sure it is OK, then slap it into the fixture, making sure it is properly seated. Then slowly lower down the drill bit to ensure the bit makes contact exactly in the center. Then drill the hole, raise the bit and remove the part and inspect it. If it is OK, put it in the container on the right."

Frank then processes a few parts, showing him how to do it and giving him the secrets and techniques found in every job. Frank then lets his brother-in-law run a few parts to acquire the skill. After observing him for a period of time and giving assistance, he tells him, "OK, I will spot check and monitor your work for the rest of the day".

At the end of the day, the brother-in-law has produced all good parts. Frank's biased and unqualified attitude has proven his point. In doing so, Frank also ruined a qualified minority applicant and contributed to the high turnover statistics.

The basic principles of 'Proper Job Instruction' are presented by Dr. Donald R. Kirkpatrick, Professor Management Development, University Extension, The University of Wisconsin,[4] for the following four step method:

Step 1—*Prepare the Worker*
      Put him at ease.
      State the job and find out what he already knows about it.
      Get him interested in learning his job.
      Place in correct position.

Step 2—*Present the Operation*

    Tell, show, and illustrate one important step at a time.

    Stress each key point.

    Instruct clearly, completely, and patiently, but no more than he can master.

Step 3—*Tryout Performance*

    Have him do the job—correct errors.

    Have him explain each key point to you as he does the job again.

    Make sure he understands.

    Continue until *YOU* know *HE* knows.

Step 4—*Follow-up*

    Put him on his own. Designate to whom he goes for help.

    Check frequently. Encourage questions.

    Taper off extra coaching and close follow-up.

The basic steps have been around for many years. These steps should be ingrained in every managers mind. However, ask your subordinate how he trains a new worker and you will find a high percentage will be unaware of the four step process.

Frequently in an attempt to be productive, the new employee suggests job improvements and cost reductions to his superior. In many such situations, the autocratic will say, "I haven't got time to listen to you. Just do the job as I told you to do it". The worker will probably try to be heard a second or third time. After that, there will be no more suggestions, because there is no positive motivation to do so. His attitude will be, it's not my problem, the boss knows it all, let him worry about it.

In our Presupervisory Assessment Programs, candidates frequently mention situations where rejected parts or products that were produced and the operator knew it, but continued because, "the boss is responsible, he has all the answers, let the boss catch it". The worker is doing the job exactly as his boss told him to do it. The boss has now created what can be described as malicious obedience and compliance. A tremendous resource has been lost. The new employee feels no responsibility and has no commitment. The problem then is not the worker, the problem is due to management's failure. A poor product or unskilled workers is not the problem—the problem is poor management.

Anxiety and stress are not caused by hard work. They are caused by a management system and organizational culture which fosters frustration, suppression, put-downs, poor communications and poor quality. Individuals attempting to treat on the job stress through stress management programs are treating the symptoms and are failing to comprehend the problem—the problem being poor management practices.

1. Donald A. Spartz, "Developing an Organization that Listens", *Manufacturing Engineering*, Volume 90, No. 3, March 1983. pp. 93-94.
2. Dr. Lawrence J. Peter, "Peter's Teacher - Education Theory", *Chicago Sun Times*, April 2, 1983.
3. "Study Finds Most Workers Unhappy With Their Firms", *Chicago Tribune*, March 12, 1982, Washington UPI.
4. Dr. Donald R. Kirkpatrick, *First-line Management* (Dearborn, Michigan: Society of Manufacturing Engineers, 1972), p. 74

3

PRINCIPLES OF DEVELOPMENT

Each year American industry spends millions of dollars to improve the skills of managers. In an attempt to develop managers, companies send select individuals to seminars, workshops, and training courses conducted by various associations, colleges, and consulting organizations.

Individuals returning from seminars typically indicate that they really enjoyed the program and thought it was worthwhile. What they are really saying is that they really enjoyed the time away from work with all expenses paid.

To say that development programs are frequently a waste of time and money is an understatement. Typically, select individuals attend a seminar, return to their plant or office and within two or three days of being back in an organizational culture where they are not permitted to apply what they have learned, they conveniently forget everything taught at the seminar. Even worse, there now may be a dissatisfied employee forced to follow management practices which he now knows are not sound. The sought after change does not take place and there is no subsequent improvement in the organization or in productivity.

Many seminars have the potential for equipping attendees with the knowledge and some of the skills necessary to institute change. Positive change, after all, should be the main reason for seminars. Those in middle and upper management who select people to attend seminars are too often the obstacles to change. They will politely listen with interest when those just returning from the seminar express new ideas and changes that ought to be considered. A typical response is that the ideas are great but now is not the time or that it would not work here. The real problem is that change is a threat to the status quo of the individual in charge.

The irony is that the manager who sent the individual to the seminar feels that he did his duty in regard to the training and development of his people. He cannot, however, understand why the individual's performance has not improved.

The Expert

In choosing development programs or seminars, one should consider the quality of the program, the instructors, and the applicability of the contents. It is not unusual to find contradictory and confusing approaches within the same seminar. In a single seminar, there may be a half dozen guest speakers who travel the circuit on a part time basis as an "expert". Attendees must select from wide variances in the approaches suggested by the different speakers. When the option is to choose from two diametrically opposed viewpoints, the middle ground, or no change from present practices, no change is always the safer choice. Even though it is healthy to have various opinions expressed, the individual should, based on change goals set in advance, develop the best approach.

Individuals attending off-premise programs are seldom in a position to select which would be best for their organization. This has already been determined by the organizational culture, climate, and the dominate management style.

A speaker at one seminar declared as a management concept, that it is better to function with autocratic clarity than it is with participative fuzziness. The line of distinction between the two will be drawn at widely different points by the autocratic person and by the participative team-oriented person.

Usually, such a statement is made by an "expert" or an individual who likes the sound of it, or deals in theory and abstractions. The tendency for the individual listening is to return to work and state that this Participative Management approach will not work. Development programs in industry do not need theory or abstractions, managers need practical proven solutions to their problems.

The discussion of varying viewpoints and concepts is important, but a company must have a good fix on the direction in which they would like to have their managers developed. This direction can be partially determined with a thorough internal analysis with a commitment to change goals. Without sound, firm direction to change goals and an organization-wide commitment to change, seminars and workshops are a waste of money.

In the past few years it has become increasingly clear that outside seminars and workshops are a thing of the past. They are entertainment-type activities. Real organizational changes can only take place when the development programs are conducted in-house with full participation, designed to meet the specific objectives of the organization and deal with the present organizational culture in relation to a sound organizational culture.

When an organization decides to spend money on training and development, change in the individual and the organization should be expected, should be demanded and programmed. The only way an organization can benefit from these development and training programs is when the change is defined in learning goals and is allowed to take place on the job through skill development with sound leadership practices. If this is stifled, the money and time is wasted; productivity and efficiency will continue to suffer and deteriorate. The small percentage of individuals who resist change through development, is in the long term, probably not capable of being developed and is certainly not affordable. With sound leadership and good management practices, people will develop, seek change, and grow.

Although learning is basic, development will not take place unless three very important principles are in place. First, the individual must recognize the *need* for learning and development. Second, the individual must *want* to learn and develop. Third, and most important, the work culture and environment *must allow* for the individual to *apply* the newly learned knowledge so that the development of skills can take place.

The Development Process

In establishing the individual's need for learning and development, the individual's immediate superior is the key. The discussion of an individual's need if undertaken at all is, however, often done in a superficial manner. Typically, individuals are invited to attend a development program or they are told to attend. Rarely are they told specifically why they should attend and the specific benefits to expect and where the organization is going. To go to a development program without preparation and without high expectations is like going to a meeting unprepared. Very little will be achieved in terms of application and results.

Although ideally, the participant's immediate superior should establish the need, it is usually through abdication and left up to the development leader to create the need in each individual. This can be accomplished by outlining the changes that are taking place in a particular field, their organization, and advising the attendees that managers will become obsolete if they do not equip themselves to cope with these changes. Changes in technology, competition, new products, a commitment to quality, and a changing workforce, are all elements of productivity and efficiency problems that might be used to establish the need for individual improvement and change. It must be real and sincere and related to the individual's job and organization.

The fact is that American industry is now at the point where it is essential that individuals recognize that if performance does not improve, if productivity has not increased in the past year in their areas of responsibility, they will become obsolete. Status quo is no longer acceptable. If output per unit of labor has not improved in the past year, then productivity has gone down. With slim profit margins, an increase in productivity, efficiency, quality and service have become must priorities and the responsibility of management.

It is often presumed, having been selected by a superior to attend a seminar or development program, that the company wants change and wants the individuals to improve their skills. While on the surface this may appear to be true, the whole exercise is a sham and waste of time and money if the management environment does not allow for change to take place. This alone answers why development programs must be conducted in-house with all participating.

In establishing the need for development, upper management cannot overlook their developmental needs. Only when upper management accepts the concepts, content and goals of the development programs in which their personnel participate and make a commitment to those programs, can change take place. The success of a development program will be in direct proportion to the organizational culture and the environment for change set by upper management. Without the commitment and involvement of upper management, the development process will fail.

In an economic downturn, training and development is often considered a "luxury" and is abolished until business improves. Communicating that training and development is a luxury is communicating a lack of commitment, a belief that training and development is not necessary and does not provide any financial return. This attitude and expectation permeates the organization. In an economic downturn, reality may indicate that training and development, like capital expenditures, must be delayed. However, like capital expenditures, it is not a luxury.

All too often the idea exists that once an individual is in management for a period of years, he does not require any further development. If an organization is to continue to evolve, then development must take place from the worker level to the CEO on a continuing basis. Some of the more successful skill development programs have been where the CEO made an appearance and/or sat in and took notes for his personal use. Most importantly, he was demonstrating interest and commitment in the development process.

Individuals with 30 years experience have at the beginning of a development program, folded their arms and stated they have heard it all before, know it all, and do not need any additional development. Usually, this individual's career consists of one year's experience—30 times over. He has the knowledge, has possibly heard it all before and unfortunately, has never applied it on the job, therefore, does not have the skills to be an effective manager.

Some training and development programs are directed to the younger workers and the outstanding performers under the assumption that the older worker has the skills or is too old to learn. The task in the '80s will be to retrain the older worker who has not acquired new skills and kept pace with technology. The alternative for the obsolete older worker is to maintain a position of substandard performance and drag one's feet until retirement, which means retirement on the job or termination. Neither of these alternatives are acceptable from a humanistic approach.

The question is often asked as to why some develop through experience while others do not. Observations indicate that many successful managers have developed new skills and greatly matured due to personal motivation and self-development. Usually, the successful manager had a model or sponsor to guide and direct his development.

The Learning Process

Obviously, before an individual can respond through learning to the areas in need of development, certain things need to take place. Individuals scheduled for development must be provided the time and guidance to put into writing some personal learning goals and how they hope to implement their development. These goals should then be reviewed within the organization to ensure they support the organization's goals. If there are clearly established goals and expectations, the results will be positive. If, on the other hand, the individual has no goals or expectations, negative or limited results will develop.

Once the learning goals and expectations have been developed, the foundation for learning has been prepared. The learning process as discussed in the chapter on "*Motivation*", is repeated here because of its importance. It involves three critical steps which must take place before an individual learns.

Acquiring Knowledge and Skill

The first step in the learning process is acquiring knowledge. Knowledge can be gained from a development program as well as from many other sources. For example, you might want to develop a college graduate to be a welder. This person can read all the books and literature on welding and acquire considerable knowledge. But does this make him qualified to do welding? Obviously, this answer is no, he will not be qualified to weld until the knowledge he possesses is applied in the welding process. He must actually weld and experience the feel and special techniques found in every job. The same applies in management. Management skills are developed through application. Knowledge, of and by itself without application, is not development, it is not learning.

The second step of the learning process is to develop the skill through actual application of the knowledge acquired. The individual must actually perform the task, get the feel of it, and develop the skills. The manager has not learned and has not developed the necessary management skills until he has applied these skills.

The third step in the learning process is the continued application of the knowledge and the development of skills until a high level of proficiency is attained. The success in the third stage will establish attitudes and behavior. Success can be measured by the individual's behavior, how well he does the job, and how he conducts himself. Is he doing the job and conducting himself more effectively than before the learning started?

Attitudes, defined as beliefs, are modified through the acquiring of knowledge and transmitted into the development of skills. Our beliefs determine our attitudes, our attitudes determine our behavior. Behavior can be modified by changing beliefs. Beliefs can be changed through acquiring knowledge and developing new skills.

Follow-up on each stage of the program is critical to ensure that when the participant leaves a session, something positive has taken place. Skills are developed through application. Therefore, follow-up is essential to ensure that change has actually been initiated. It also becomes increasingly apparent that from a cost benefit standpoint, the most effective approach toward development is where the entire management staff is involved. The learning process ties directly to the proper four step job instruction outlined in the previous chapter.

How many times during the past few years have you heard the statement: "We are losing all of our skilled and dedicated workers." Some thought is necessary to explain why this has happened.

Take a typical group of ten employees all working for a single manager. Within the group he will have two skilled key employees he depends on during an emergency, a crisis, a rush or a difficult job. This same manager will complain that when these two key individuals retire, he will lose all of his skilled workers. Ask him why he never permitted his other employees to acquire the skills to do the emergency job, handle the crisis, the rush or the difficult job, and his response will be he "never had the time" to let them do it. Unfortunately, if he never lets the individual do the job and acquire the necessary skills, they will never be able to become skilled workers. As a result, a mediocre work force is developed.

Industry is losing skilled workers because of reliance on a few select skilled workers and a failure to develop the total work force to be more productive. It is a form of favoritism. At some stage, time must be taken to develop all the workers that have the capability to learn. Some of the restrictive job descriptions prevent new skill development. The sooner management and labor recognize this and eliminate restrictive job descriptions, the sooner productivity will improve.

This same learning process must be recognized in the development of supervisors and managers. Supervisors and managers learn by acquiring knowledge and applying it on the job until they have their skills firmly entrenched. The supervisor and manager with the proper knowledge and skills will then demonstrate the desired behavior. This behavior will result in improving productivity.

It is difficult to cultivate this basic practice. It is too easy in a crisis or rush job to assign it to "the busy person". Busy people don't make excuses—they execute. It is best to keep everybody busy with new and challenging learning experiences. Busy people can always do one more assignment. People with only one assignment immediately complain about the second.

The discussion on the principle of development requires some suggestions on how to effectively manage development. Meaningful development is based on organizational and individual goals. Both short and long-term goals must be in writing, be attainable, measurable, have a completion date, and agreed on by the individuals involved. These goals then lead to the plan(s) on how the goals will be achieved. Essential to success is a commitment by the CEO to development, attainment of the goals, and the plan to achieve this.

A commitment must be communicated by beliefs, believing in the development process, involvement, and actions which support and reinforce the process. This does not mean that the goals and the plan are set in concrete. In an on-going development process, as problems, conflicts, challenges, new ideas and concepts develop, the Participative Team Manager must listen, and be open to change the goals and plans. Skill development in capitalizing on creativity, innovative ideas, problems, conflicts, and challenging present practices and policies, is the Participative Team Management approach. The Participative Team Supervisor-Manager is always seeking the best ideas and solutions regardless of the source.

In the development process, the goals, plans, and the commitment are basic. Successful organizations have found it desirable to establish a Development Center. Ideally, this should be a facility where the environment is conducive to group meetings and small task forces working on specific development opportunities. The facility center is strongly suggested. The Development Center, whether a physical setting or a concept and practice, will be the trend in the '80s.

In 1961 while working with the Boeing Company in Seattle, considerable emphasis was placed on research and development. Boeing had a physical Development Center where an engineer, a scientist, or a supervisor-manager with an idea was given the time and support to develop and prove theory, concepts, and practices. Development in their industry meant survival. This same development concept means survival in any industry.

The Development Center should be geared to develop people at all levels, i.e., to develop sales, strategic market development, product development, production improvement, goals, and to develop the Standards of Performance used to identify each individuals responsibilities and performance, and the conditions that will exist when a job is well done and acceptable to his supervisor. It means the development of the organization as a whole.

4

CREATING AN ENVIRONMENT FOR CHANGE

What we did yesterday is probably not good enough today. The revitalization and development of a sound organizational culture is accomplished by educating and teaching managers to manage more effectively with Participative Team Management concepts and practices. The education and teaching of managers needs to be based on sound principles of human behavior which seek creative changes in developing effective leaders.

Success in the revitalization and development process requires an understanding that people do not, contrary to general beliefs, resist change. Through effective leadership, people want change, need change, and will seek change. Resistance to change or acceptance of status quo develops under ineffective leadership. An ineffective manager creates resistance through unsound practices and failure to obtain trust and respect. The economic loss resulting from so-called resistance to change, the fear to ask questions, report problems, resolve conflicts and communicate openly without fear, is high.

Creating an environment of change means being able to develop an environment of not necessarily doing it today the same way it was done yesterday. The environment must be one of trust, respect, and responsibility with the ability to voice an opinion at any time.

Creating change for the development of a sound organizational culture requires an understanding of present attitudes and concepts as to what constitutes effective leadership and management. This requires an evaluation which will cause an organization to change its leadership and management styles toward a participative team relationship. This sounds very easy; however, how many managers recognize or acknowledge that they are not open to change? Change is difficult when our mind is closed due to ineffective leadership.

The Process of Change

How can change take place in individuals and in organizations? There are two prerequisites. First, the need to change must be recognized and accepted; and second, the leadership involved must have sound leadership skills, which will cause others to seek change. When these two elements are present, the process of change can begin.

The next question is, "Where should change begin?" Should change begin at the top of an organization, at the first line level of supervision, or somewhere in-between? The textbooks tell us that change must start at the top with the Chairman and President. Unfortunately, most textbook writers work in a sterile environment and have not encountered the real world.

Obviously, the involvement, support, and commitment of top management is essential. However, the process can start at any level provided top management is involved, committed, and demonstrates a style of management that will project openness, receptivity, and a willingness to listen. The process should simultaneously start with top management and procede down through and including the first line supervisors. The process however, can start from the bottom up with first line supervisors. It is in fact, desirable, since first line supervisors need to acquire the basic management skills prior to becoming involved in Participative Team Management development. The greatest barrier in the process of change is the failure to understand the process of creating change by developing trust and respect with open communications.

A heavy equipment manufacturer attempted to bring about internal change by obtaining more employee participation and involvement. A 20-year company veteran of middle management status was given the title Manager of Development, with the responsibility to design, implement, and coordinate the process. This individual had heard and read about the most recent fad, the quality control circle (QCC) group approach and considered it the answer. He attended a seminar on the subject, became an "expert", and developed his program. His approach was to meet with workers in small groups and obtain their ideas and problems. In the process, he bypassed the workers' immediate supervisor and middle management which created resistance and resentment. He was exposing problems supervisors and middle management had been suppressing, were aware of, and probably created. He also failed to obtain top management's understanding of the process and their commitment to change. Management was verbally saying yes, we want change; however, they continued their autocratic and adversarial style of management.

The workers in the QCC groups immediately sensed this contradiction and rejected the Manager of Development along with the entire QC program. His experience and expertise in understanding the process of change was absent. He failed to comprehend that an organization's culture must be supportive of change, if change is to be genuine and authentic. Change in this case could not take place until the autocratic and adversarial style of management was altered throughout the organization.

Problems in achieving results in development programs usually occur because of the piecemeal approach. A comprehensive plan is lacking and the development is always left to someone else. Supervisors and managers are sent to numerous outside courses, seminars or workshops. When they return to the existing leadership styles and organizational culture, they must forget all they have heard and supposedly learned while attending these sessions. They are "trained"; however, due to the existing organizational culture and practices, no change takes place.

Improvement cannot take place without applying the knowledge the individual has acquired. Application of this knowledge is discouraged in the process of maintaining the status quo.

Outside seminars etc., have generally proven to be ineffective in creating change. John Humble, an international expert in Time Management seminars refers to these popular one day seminars as strictly "time entertainment". They are a waste of time since no organizational change will evolve as a result of these seminars. This is true with the multitude of public seminars conducted by the theory and gimmick experts.

Time Management, Participative Team Management and Supervisory Skill Development involves a very complex, organized, systematic process to bring about organizational change. The development leader must possess a high degree of expertise if change is to actually take place and productivity is to improve through a revitalized organization.

Revitalized management and organizational change for increased productivity means a total development program from the top executive down to and including first line supervisors. To change means to move from the traditional types of management systems to an organizational culture consisting of recognition and involvement with Participative Team Management concepts and practices. It means change from the autocratic, the do-nothing type, the pleasing procrastinator, and the indecisive bureaucratic style of management. This cannot take place in one day, a week or a month.

Revitalizing management is a complex process where new skills must be acquired over a period of time. The task for the executive is to set a course of action based on goals and a plan for change and revitalization of the individuals and the organizational culture. Recognizing that many prefer status quo, the executive must have a firmly established plan in order to initiate change. Resistance to organizational changes in management practices will come from the very individuals that have discouraged change through their adversarial practices.

The process of change should be carefully planned and communicated. The planning should start with change goals, and an action plan with a timetable. A one to three year program is suggested, depending on the present existing organizational culture. In actual practice, complete revitalization will take between five and ten years.

John Galvin, CEO, at Motorola Inc. states: "The organization has been working toward Participative Management for 13 years...40% are in place, with hopes that they will have the other 60% ready in two years". Galvin goes on to say: "If industry does not develop Participative Management practices within the next 10 years they will have to lock the doors".

A Strategic Revitalization and Development Plan, designed to create change, should be a phased program. There are no short cuts in the process. The program must be specific, dynamic, and provide the guidelines with check points for measurement and communication with feedback to all parties involved. The program must be tailored to each organization's needs and goals. A typical plan is outlined below:

PHASE I

Identifying Present Status and Establishment of the Long Range Plan
> Define the Organizational Needs.
> Define the Organizational Goals.
> Define the Individual Development Needs.
> Develop an Organizational Development Plan.
> Establish Concurrent Critique Procedures.

PHASE II

Details on Implementing the Plan
> Selecting the Programs to Achieve the Goals.
> Selecting the Participants and Scheduling.
> Establishing Responsibilities for Implementing the Plan.

PHASE III

Implementation
> Supervisory Skill Development.
> Standards of Performance.
> Participative Team Management.
> Management by Objectives.

PHASE IV

Worker Involvement

Productivity Improvement Groups.

PHASE V

Identify Developmental Status with Feedback to Phase I

Monitoring and Measuring Results.

Retraining and Reinforcement Sessions.

Redefining the Organization's and Management Development Needs.

Feedback to Phase I.

PHASE I

Define the Organizational Needs. The initial process of defining the organization's needs is often extremely difficult. In addition, the needs as initially perceived may deal only with symptoms of the problems. If each member of management were to define the organization's needs, they would be based on each individual's personal beliefs, assumptions and interests. Each individual will perceive the needs of an organization differently, and there is a high probability that the needs will not reveal the real problem.

A CEO has a constant need to improve the bottom line. The Sales Manager must increase sales, the Quality Control Manager has a need to cut down on rejects, and the Production Manager must increase output. The CEO may forego expenditures to achieve short-term results, the Sales Manager wants another salesman, the Quality Control Manager wants another inspector, and production wants to hire more people. The problem may be perceived that the worker is not building quality into the product. To the worker, the problem may be an adversarial climate, poor supervision, poor equipment, job restrictions, and those people "up front".

In advance of attending our Participative Team Management program, participants are asked to develop seven critical problems, based on priority, that are suppressing productivity within their organization. The first three problems usually include communications, cooperation and management attitudes. The remainder of the problems often reflect individual interest and needs. In reality all of these problems may only be symptoms, with the organization's management practices, the climate, and the culture being the real problem.

The organizational needs will easily and very specifically be definable once the Standards of Performance, and goals and objectives are in effect throughout an organization for a period of time. In addition, these developmental needs are highlighted when Participative Team Management practices are in effect.

Define the Organizational Developmental Goals. Organizational goal setting is a step which is often overlooked, yet it is basic to the process. Identification of organizational needs permits establishment of measurable goals. The goals permit development of a plan to achieve the goals. Too often when the goals are defined by the Executive Group, only a very small percentage of the goals are communicated down to the first line level of management. First line managers perceive this lack of involvement as being excluded as a part of management, or because they are not trustworthy. Consequently, first line managers develop corresponding negative behavioral patterns which are then interpreted by upper management as not being trustworthy, thus completing the self-fulfilling prophecy.

Define the Individual Development Needs. Defining and writing individual development needs is difficult in the early phase. It is difficult to determine someone else's needs, and often more difficult to determine and admit one's personal development needs. As a consequence, these needs must initially be determined in fairly broad terms for each member of management. The need may be determined to be in either communications or motivation. With the first line level of management there may be a need for discipline, job instruction techniques, or quality. These are areas which do not require any individual to recognize they personally have a problem, since they can always blame the problem on someone else.

Generally, people tend to deal with the symptoms and fail to identify the real problem or the contributing causes. The plant superintendent will complain about his supervisors not keeping him informed or not meeting production/quality standards. These are usually symptoms of a much deeper problem. The real problem is usually the organizational culture, the climate, and management practices imposed from above by the plant superintendent.

It is, however, a starting point, and will eventually in Phase III, lead to determining specific individual development needs. Individual development needs must be constantly redefined and upgraded in the revitalization process to reflect the rapid changes which will occur.

Without written goals, an organization and an individual will simply wander. Individuals and organizations without a goal have nothing to accomplish, have no direction, no priorities, and will not know when or where they have gone. Certainly without a goal there is a need to plan, since goals must precede planning.

Managers, supervisors and workers frequently state that they put in their eight hours and do a fair day's work for their pay and leave. These individuals are actually saying that they have no goals, no purpose, except to do enough to get by. They have not been motivated in the proper direction.

The importance of establishing organizational and individual career and work goals has long been advocated. The use of goals as a way of managing, unfortunately, has not taken place. The general feeling is, "I don't need goals, it's the other guy who needs goals". In development sessions we ask, who has a goal? Out of a group of 20 participants, there will usually be two or three individuals that respond. If we then ask who has their goals in writing, seldom will there be a single response. Out of the thousands of supervisors and middle managers completing our skills program, less than 5% have indicated they have a goal in writing.

The setting of goals is simple. Goals must be in writing, measurable and attainable, with a specified time frame for accomplishing these goals that has been agreed on between the superior and the subordinate. The results to be achieved should exceed the normal job requirements. Achieving normal job requirements as defined by the Standards of Performance should be considered only average performance. Average performance of meeting one's standards should mean an individual gets to keep his job and receive an average pay raise.

Can you imagine the pilot of a 747 leaving Chicago for Dallas without a goal in writing and a flight plan in order to achieve his goal and arrive safely at Dallas within a predetermined time? Can you imagine a supervisor, a manager, or an executive who is responsible for human, capital, and natural resources working without current written goals? Can you imagine a first level manager, a clerical worker, or a machine operator working without goals?

Develop a Strategic Organizational Development Plan. Goals must come first to establish direction and the desired result. The plan establishes how the goals will be achieved. The development plan should detail how and when the goals will be achieved and who will be responsible.

Concurrent Critique. A productive management practice establishes the practice of concurrent self-critiquing of progress on a continuous basis. A concurrent critique is defined as critiquing performance as a management practice and confirming and/or adjusting the continued course of action. It should become a habit in a development program as in any management function, to periodically stop and critique performance. Someone needs to ask whether progress is being made, is the plan on schedule, is this a sound approach, are goals being met? If the answers are negative, the individual or the group needs to determine why and make the necessary corrections and/or adjustments. Such corrections cannot wait until the end of the program or at the conclusion of a production run—when failure becomes fact.

PHASE II

Selecting the Programs to Achieve the Goals. Phase I encompassed the definition of the organizational needs, including the development of the organizational development goals, defining the individual development needs, establishing a strategic development plan, and the concurrent critique of the various elements of the phase. Selecting the specific revitalization programs in Phase II is now an easy process. The revitalization program then must be designed to fit the specific needs of the organization and the individuals.

One problem which is prevalent is the lack of supervisory and management skills at the first and middle management levels. These must be acquired prior to developing a sound organization culture through Participative Team Building activities. As a consequence, the first step may be to determine, verify, and profile the necessary skills for first and middle levels of management. This involves profiling the skills a job requires and the existing skills of supervisory personnel. This will establish the developmental gap which can be eliminated through a training and development program.

There is however, a negative side to this approach. Profiling required skills without the Standards of Performance is questionable. In actual practice, a Supervisory Skill Development program and the Standards of Performance can be completed quickly and at less cost then "attempting" to profile required skills. The academics and theory experts don't like this since they prefer a detailed time-consuming profile project. The Standards of Performance provides a bases for identifying specific individual development needs.

Selecting the Participants. The completion of the development and organizational needs in Phase I along with the identification of the needed program also makes the selection of participants apparent. If an organization is to change and become revitalized, the development of all individuals is essential. Every member of management, including administrative, operational, and staff support must be included in the development process. However, the development needs vary significantly between individuals. This means that the revitalization plan will be a long-term process to bring about the revitalization of management and the development of a sound organizational culture.

Selecting and Implementing the Plan. Implementation of the program requires that a task group or someone be assigned the responsibility to

34

manage the revitalization program. The individual should be open and candid, a good listener, possess good communication skills, be able to establish goals, and continue to seek the best solution for the organization as a team. He must set priorities, question, challenge, and at the same time create a sense of urgency in the program. He must also be able to obtain and maintain a commitment and involvement by key executives to support the plan. The individual selected to implement the program must be progressive and in a position to make decisions, and at the same time maintain a relatively low profile. The individual should be the catalyst for change and not the director of change. The individual must also be skilled in working with various management styles, must be able to identify resistance, quiet sabotage, and then move quickly to ensure that the program continues.

PHASE III

Supervisory Skill Development. The process of developing supervisors with sound skills can start with an Assessment Program to identify and select potential entry level supervisors. This is done via a program designed to identify employees with supervisory potential. Each candidate can be assessed for ability and potential in a series of activities which include: problem identification and analysis, judgement, decisiveness, leadership, interpersonal sensitivity, initiative and organizational planning. All are qualities which are essential in becoming an effective member of management.

A second step in the Supervisory Skill Development program should be a comprehensive program designed to develop effective skilled supervisors. Supervisors need to participate in intensive exercises and conflict situations designed to help each individual develop and acquire the necessary basic supervisory skills along with positive attitudes and expectations.

There are some barriers in developing supervisory skills. I recall meeting with a Plant Superintendent on a skills program I was preparing to start with his organization. He was an autocratic manager who did not believe in training his personnel beyond what he was capable of, and did not want any help. The program had been contracted by the CEO. Involvement and commitment by the Plant Superintendent was essential. The Superintendent expressed his concern in reviewing the program elements in one major area— problem identification and solving. In the course of the program, each participant would identify a problem, work it through the solution process and present it to the group which would later present it to management, including the Plant Superintendent. The Superintendent's statement was, "You are going to stir things up, you scare the hell out of me". It took time to understand his reasoning. His fear was in having the problems which he had spent years suppressing, identified and presented to his superiors. The organization's developmental goals and commitment had not been properly communicated to the Plant Superintendent.

Standards of Performance. The next step in the Supervisory Skill Development program is the development and installation of the Standards of Performance. First level supervisors, certain middle managers and clerical personnel often have difficulty identifying their responsibilities, how well they must perform, what is expected of them, and how their performance will be evaluated. The Standards of Performance identify each individuals responsibilities and establish performance standards. A standard is developed for each responsibility which then provides a means to objectively measure performance. Most importantly, the standard permits the individual to set priorities, and to plan and achieve measurable results. A standard is defined as the condition that will exist when a responsibility is well done and acceptable to the individuals immediate superior. The Standards of Performance are discussed at length in Chapter 7 entitled *"Measuring Individual Productivity and Standards of Performance"*.

Participative Team Management. The development of Participative Team Management (PTM) is the most important phase in the development of a sound organizational culture. Participative Team Management is designed to develop sound management practices and attitudes within a good environment. Participants develop team management skills with the ability to identify and work with the different individual styles of management.

Team skills means the development of a nonadversarial working relationship throughout the organization. Restrictive job responsibilities are identified and challenged with individuals working together as a team to improve communications, identify and solve problems, and face and resolve conflicts rather than "sweeping them under the carpet". All are essential elements to develop a sound organizational culture and to consistently achieve profit and productivity goals.

In Participative Team Management, each individual identifies and becomes aware of his leadership style and the impact it has on other members of the team. Participants become more open, more receptive and more candid in their communications. The barriers are minimized with participants working to help each other achieve organizational goals, while also achieving and maintaining a high performance in individual job responsibilities. This subject is discussed in Chapter 12 entitled *"Participative Team Management Skills"*.

Management by Objectives. While the Standards of Performance are effective with first line and middle managers, Management by Objectives (MBO) works well with middle and upper management people, and with people with highly technical jobs including Research and Development people. These individuals must have the freedom to act, to be creative, and to concentrate on the few vital activities that make the difference in an organization.

Management by Objectives has faltered in the past years due to poorly developed and administered programs. Management by Objectives was used as an attempt to achieve results without developing a sound organizational culture. Consequently, the MBO process failed. Supervisors and mid-level managers without the Standards of Performance, discovered that with MBO, they could concentrate on the three or four objectives to the neglect of their normal basic essential responsibilities. As a result, many of the necessary basic activities were not properly covered. Acceptable performance of an individual's basic job should come first with the objectives being over and above the Standards of Performance.

PHASE IV

Productivity Improvement Groups. This phase is designed to have supervisors and managers meet with, listen to, and obtain the workers' ideas and suggestions on improving productivity. The concept is not new. For years managers-supervisors have been involving employees by listening, training and participation in employee group meetings. Quality circles was an attempt to obtain employee participation. What was new about the quality circle being lifted and adopted from the Japanese culture, was the formal approach. This approach was essentially self-serving to the orginator and his future job security. The attempt to use QCC's failed and has caused long-term damage. The quality circle approach failed because Participative Team Management concepts and practices were not in place and organizational cultures were not sound. There is, however, still a need for worker productivity improvement groups.

There are a number of conditions which must exist for worker involvement and participation to succeed. If this approach is to be successful, the supervisor or manager must possess the necessary leadership skills. He must be skilled in conducting meetings, he must have the skill to effectively listen and ask questions, and he must also possess the necessary skill of knowing how to implement and funnel the participant's recommendations and suggestions, including the ability to tell the participants why their suggestions or recommendations would not be feasible. Our experience indicates that when PTM concepts and practices are in place, worker involvement is also in place, and listening to employees is a normal activity. Consequently, QCC's are then not necessary.

Most importantly, the organizational culture must be sound or the program of worker involvement will fail. Participative Team Management development which is designed to create a sound organizational culture, should precede worker productivity improvement groups.

PHASE V

Monitoring and Measuring Results. All programs that are worthy of being implemented should be measurable for results achieved in improving productivity. Difficulty in measuring results may be caused by the fact that there presently is no means by which to measure productivity. If organizations do not currently have a measurement plan, it will be almost impossible to accurately measure improvement in the future. First line supervisors, office support personnel and middle management people can be effectively and objectively measured using the Standards of Performance approach.

Senior and middle management can be effectively measured with predetermined goals and objectives. The measurement of productivity of a unit is essential to ensure that the organization's goals, service, quality, or research and development are achieved.

Retraining and Reinforcement Session. One of the problems in any development program is that people learn and retain at different levels. In addition, skills can be lost and behavior patterns can change. As a result, retraining and reinforcement sessions need to be developed and scheduled. These sessions should be directed at the specific needs of individuals. The programs can be in group sessions where the needs are identified, or on a one-on-one basis of coaching to meet the specific needs of an individual.

Redefining the Organization's and Management Development Needs. With the completion and measurement of results of the programs designed to meet the needs of the organization, the development needs can then be redefined more specifically for an on-going development process. In each phase, specific individual needs are identified. The identification of specific needs means that an organization can now concentrate on actual needs versus assuming everyone has a need for a program on communications. The organization's needs will change as new goals are established.

Feedback to PHASE I. Finally, the acknowledged emerging basic needs can then be looped back to start the development process over again as a new

Phase I. At this point, the hidden contributing causes can be addressed with specific programs and actions to change. Development and learning is a continuous, never ending process. The individual who has ceased to learn, expand, and who claims to know it all, is obsolete in our present working environment.

People do not naturally resist change—people want change. People do naturally resist poor leadership, the feeling of being used, suppressed and put down. Change can then only take place where the climate is open and leadership is sound. Revitalization and development programs are a method of bringing about change with the development of sound management skills and practices.

5

SUPERVISION

The term "supervision" is generally associated with first line activities. It is usually not construed to be synonymous with "management". Supervision exists at all levels of the management system and the problems and principles are essentially identical.

The entry level supervisor has been referred to as the key person, has been provided the minimal amount of training, and is referred to as the problem. This is the job where habits, attitudes and practices are acquired and often carried through an individual's lifetime.

A few highly motivated individuals in the entry level group will grow through self-development. A few will grow by having a sponsor to provide the extra guidance, coaching and skills. The remaining individuals which constitute the majority, will tend to wander and provide mediocre performance.

Entry level management positions have traditionally been filled with individuals selected from the ranks. In the past, they were often selected because they possessed the necessary technical skill, were productive workers, and maintained a good attendance record. More than likely, some of these people were also chosen because of their compliant, cooperative, nondisruptive, conforming attitude. The person is chosen because he is not considered to be a threat to the boss.

The traditional managers have been successful in selecting subordinates they can control and trust. As a result, these managers often developed supervisors and a labor force, which ironically, they themselves label as mediocre when the going is tough. There is a need for people who challenge, are creative, and question the present in order to seek improvement.

Managers continue to appoint and promote subordinates who are images of themselves. This assures the traditional ineffective manager that the new appointee will not pose a threat, and will not bring about change. This climate creates an atmosphere where conflicts are not resolved, problems are concealed, communications are poor, and improvements are discouraged. A lack of imagination suppresses creativity and change becomes even more difficult. As a result, the organizational culture becomes stagnant.

Many middle managers come from first line supervisory ranks and are not well prepared. Many do not, without considerable development, have the capability to devise improvements or to produce quality products or services. This is a serious problem which requires new direction with strong leadership from the top to select and develop better and stronger leadership at the bottom. Even though supervisors and managers in the white-collar field may have extensive educational backgrounds, their leadership skills have not been proportionately developed.

Supervision today is a new job, a field which has very little relationship to the job of a skilled worker or lead person. Unfortunately, newly appointed supervisors-managers receive little or no training to develop skills needed for the new job. Many times they are informed on Friday that they will become supervisors-managers on Monday. These soon-to-be supervisors-managers are completely unprepared, do not know how to plan or regulate the work flow, do not know how to maintain quality, and are unfamiliar with controlling waste. Nor do they know how to conduct an interview, select or train people. Motivation, communication, coaching, counseling and job instruction skills are often lacking. These new supervisors do not know how to handle employee complaints, nor do they know how to deal with adversarial situations. They may not even know the meaning of the word productivity.

The status of entry level supervisors-managers is low at best. Employees generally give guarded recognition for their status. As a result, many will decline a promotion to the supervisory ranks. Supervisors themselves may have a poor self-image. They tend to see their role, based on examples, as a buffer or insulator between employees, middle, and upper management.

Many functions once controlled by supervisors have been eroded over the years by other departments. The Personnel Department hires, disciplines, promotes, and fires. Quality Control inspects. Maintenance repairs. Schedulers tell him what and when. Coordinators, planners and efficiency experts fine tune. Engineering purchases equipment. Finance pays. The reason given for taking away some of these functions is a lack of supervisory skills, which is the result of failing to properly select and develop good supervisors.

The remaining functions consist of the responsibility to expedite the production process. In limbo and not feeling a part of management or of belonging to the work force, the supervisor tends to identify more closely with the work force rather than with management, although he is not fully accepted by either. As a consequence, he attempts to lead by establishing friendships which further compromises his fragile position of leadership.

The Questionnaire

At the beginning of a Management Supervisory Skill Development Program, each participant completes a Questionnaire. One of the questions asks for a definition of the term "management". This question has produced some very interesting responses. The respondents had all been in supervision for a number of years with some having 30 years or more supervisory duties. The following are some typical responses provided from first line supervisors and middle managers:

- "Manipulate employees to make a profit."
- "The head of the snake, without them to direct and lead, the tail can go nowhere."
- "Decision making body which delegates to his supervisors what they want done."
- "Respect, not aggravate, and do what is supposed to be done on time."
- "People who direct to achieve production goals."
- "Top line force."
- "To create no problems that cut production."
- "A business that runs for profit."
- "Making money through people and equipment in a safe manner."
- "The President of the company."
- "Top Brass."
- "Persons who set back, give orders, and have people under him do the job."
- "Any person who is in charge of a group of people and takes the blame for everything that goes wrong."
- "A person who watches over the supervisor."
- "They are and always will be the bosses of any company."

There are some good answers; however, based on the responses on the Questionnaire over the past 10 years, 73% of the supervisors-managers did not consider themselves a part of management; 13% considered themselves a part of management; and the remaining 14% didn't know where they stood as they had no opinion about the question. It was apparent from the responses that a high percentage of first line supervisors and some middle managers do not consider themselves a part of management. They may have been verbally told they are a part of management; however, actions by their superiors and other managers spoke louder than words.

Selection of Supervisors-Managers

There are indeed many excellent first line supervisors. Others might be considered average and some are not qualified to perform their roles in carrying out their responsibilities. Nonetheless, it is unjust to place blame on the unqualified supervisor. In many situations, they have been placed in their present positions with little consideration as to their leadership or inter-personal skills. In addition, very little assistance or opportunities are provided for skill development.

A client, being extremely unhappy with his supervisory staff and their inability to train, discipline, enforce work rules, obtain quality work, or to motivate and communicate, requested an Assessment Program to select qualified supervisory-management candidates. The client realized that in the past, individuals had been promoted into the supervisory ranks due to their record of being good, reliable, production employees. The recognition that many of his supervisors were not suited to their roles and after considerable training were still ineffective, prompted the request for an objective assessment of his potential managers.

The plant manager and the line supervisors selected 20 individuals to participate in a two-day Assessment Program. Two of these individuals—lead persons—had already been privately promised a supervisory position, a fact unknown to the assessors. At the conclusion of the two-day program, the three assessors met to compare their findings. Each had been independently assessing the individuals without discussion between the other assessors. All three evaluators had assessed the two individuals that had been promised supervisory positions and according to their evaluations, were at the bottom of their lists of potential supervisory candidates. These two individuals were not recommended for promotion into supervision.

Cloning

The supervisors who had selected these two individuals, were themselves recognized as being ineffective by their superiors. They had selected these individuals because they were clones of themselves. The supervisors had selected individuals they could easily control and who would not be a threat or disruptive to the operation. The typical supervisory selection process virtually guarantees that new entries will be identical to those that are doing the selecting. No new ideas will be forthcoming. Certainly there will be no changes and ineffectiveness will continue.

44

We are reminded of a Personnel Manager who had been with a company for over 30 years and was excessively overweight. He was responsible for hiring all the clerical employees. It was amazing to walk through the offices and see all the employees of his same physical stature and attire.

The positive side is when effective supervisors and managers select new supervisors like themselves. Effective managers will probably select individuals who will also be effective. High expectations of oneself and of the new supervisor will produce positive results. Negative expectations in the selection process will produce negative results. The unfortunate aspect is that many poor supervisors and managers consider themselves effective. There is a high degree of self-deception in all of us.

A review of our records developed from a number of Assessment Programs indicate that only one out of ten lead persons evaluated in all of the programs was assessed as a qualified candidate for supervision. The Assessment Programs have clearly indicated the fallacy that exists in the automatic practice of promoting lead persons into supervisory positions. The practice fails to differentiate between the role of the lead person and that of the supervisor. The lead person displays distinctive characteristics of functioning on a one-on-one basis and usually possesses a high degree of technical skills. The duties of the supervisor are quite different. While the supervisor must have adequate technical knowledge, his most important role becomes that of teacher, planner, advisor and consultant.

The purpose of a sound supervisory assessment and selection program was summed up in the statement by the CEO's of two separate organizations:

"In the past we have not done a good job in selecting entry level managers. I intend to change that by having an objective assessment with a Skill Development Program so we will have qualified and skilled managers in the future."

"Our entire intention is to objectively select and train, before the need arises, suitable management candidates so that when the vacancy does occur, someone will be properly trained to assist in management."

The Role of Supervision

The role of the supervisor-manager is to develop and maintain a productive work force. In order for a worker to achieve an adequate level of productivity, he must be able to take total responsibility for his job. The workers must be provided the opportunity for self-expression and creativity. The worker must be allowed to contribute some intellectual innovation that stimulates the imagination. Ideas must receive consideration and if feasible, be implemented with proper credit and recognition given for the contribution.

The effective supervisor recognizes that he must create the proper climate, be fair, firm, and consistent in all phases of his activities. Along with technical skills, he must possess leadership skills and a sound understanding of interpersonal relationships. Goals must be established and he must be able to create a sense of urgency in reaching them. He must also understand the attitudes of employees and be able to modify both attitudes and behavior to obtain the desired worker behavior. The successful supervisor also recognizes that the attitudes and beliefs of the employees in the work place are a direct reflection of his attitudes and beliefs and those of his superiors.

The supervisor must be attentive to feedback, evaluate performance and provide opportunities for continuous learning and growth. The qualities possessed by a supervisor who is effective in this regard include that of being a casual observer and a good listener. If individuals are freed from the restraint of over-supervision and autocratic control, workers and supervisors will develop creative and productive approaches to their work.

Unless the work environment and the management style is responsive to worker input, individuals and work groups cannot reasonably be expected to seek out new responsibilities and carry them out in a productive way. Certainly, this response will not be forthcoming by demand. If the worker is not given the opportunity to contribute input into the decision making process and is not to be heard, creativity will be stifled and there will be no incentive to do more than the absolute minimum. Eventually, the worker will not be motivated to participate and will lose the ability and enthusiasm to think and make the simplest of decisions.

Supervisors should be expected not only to assume responsibility for their individual jobs but also to assume a responsibility for the work group, its relationship to the work process, its structure, and its cohesiveness. In this process, the supervisor is a resource to the work group. A resource is defined as: "Something that lies ready for use or that can be drawn upon for aid or to take care of a need, to be able to deal promptly and effectively with problems and conflicts". Far from being a qualified lead person, the function today requires that supervisors have the knowledge and ability to effectively place, train, motivate and communicate with employees, to develop high standards through worker participation, and to provide guidance in a wide range of areas.

The Planning Period

One of the major functions of first line supervision is planning. In an economic downturn, we hear that the problem in our management system is short-term versus long-term planning. This is partially true with top management; however, first line supervisors must be skilled in short-term planning. First line supervision must be concerned with what happened during the last shift, what is happening in the current shift, what will happen in the next 24 hours, and during the current month and quarter. The first line supervisor must use his hour-by-hour responsibility to assign and monitor the incremented flow of detailed work throughout his area of responsibility. This means the first line manager must be well trained, alert and attentive.

The planning period differs from being short and long-term at the top of an organization to very short-term at the lower level of an organization. The essential element is a goal. As discussed in an earlier chapter and at the end of this chapter, goals must precede planning. Without a goal we wander. Without a goal, the first line supervisor cannot plan properly and will appropriately be labeled as an expeditor or an individual who takes care of brush fires.

Surveys indicate that supervisors dislike the task of disciplining. The very use of the word discipline has negative implications and creates barriers. The term must be put into a positive framework. To discipline is to correct an individual's work habits and behavior. To correct an individual is to train the worker in safe and productive work habits. Disciplinary actions are necessary when all attempts at 'training' and 'correcting' have failed. The disciplinary skills of being fair, firm and consistent, leads to respect and acceptance.

Douglas McGregor's book, *The Human Side of Enterprise*[1] with his Theory X and Theory Y, presented fundamental choices for managing workers and for working. Theory X, the traditional management approach to workers and working, assumes that people are lazy, dislike and shun work, have to be driven and need both the carrot and the stick. This theory also assumes that most people are incapable of taking responsibility for themselves and have to be looked after. Under the traditional approach, autocratic managers base their action on Theory X assumptions in managing the workers. McGregor's Theory Y is essentially the opposite of Theory X.

The Individual's Needs

The autocratic manager relates to the first three human needs as developed by Maslow.[2] These are the physiological needs, the safety and security needs, and the love and social needs. What the traditional manager does not understand is that once an employee is hired and has survived beyond the probationary period, these basic needs are essentially fulfilled. While these needs were at one time a motivating factor, once fulfilled, they are no longer motivational. The autocratic supervisor is then rendered outmoded and ineffective and his adversarial approach using fear and threat tactics compound the problem.

Knowledgeable, skilled supervisors and managers realize the greater motivational aspects in the other levels of Maslow's hierarchy of needs. The fourth need, self-esteem, reaches levels of great importance once the basic needs are fulfilled. In fulfilling the need for self-respect and self-esteem of others, people respond to the individual's desire for strength, adequacy, confidence, reputation, prestige, recognition, attention and appreciation. Rarely are these needs completely satisfied. The individual's need for recognition is what makes the person attract attention to himself and if not permitted in a positive manner, this need will be displayed by negative behavior. The individual wants his points, motives, actions or intentions to be noticed and accepted not only by his superiors, but also his peers. These are all motivational aspects that the supervisor must be aware of and be able to respond to in the motivation of employees.

The recession of 1982-83 has given some temporary reassurance to the traditional manager. One has only to listen to workers who have been laid off for one to two years and then recalled. These workers are glad to be working and state they will work harder and produce better quality goods. Prior to the lay off, these individuals were seeking self-esteem and self-fulfillment. After being laid off and then recalled, they are now back in Maslow's hierarchy physiological need (food, shelter, etc.) and the need for safety and security. As the economy improves and as these needs are satisfied, the individuals will revert to the needs of self-esteem and self-fulfillment. Managers now have the time to prepare and meet this challenge through Participative Team Management concepts and practices.

In helping employees fulfill the need for self-esteem, the supervisor's role will change from enforcing, disciplining, controlling and directing to a role of assisting, planning, training, guiding, motivating and honestly communicating. The terminology will continue to change from authority to responsibilities and what can be contributed to the organization. By listening to employees, obtaining their ideas and gaining their involvement and commitment, important progress can be made in responding to these needs. The greatest resource for information is from the worker. The problem is that few present day supervisors either do not recognize the resource of this knowledge or are forced to ignore it because of the organizational culture.

Where absenteeism, tardiness, poor quality, rejects and safety problems are found, there is usually a dominate autocratic management style present.

These are problems that are caused by ineffective management. The autocratic manager's belief and expectations that employees are lazy and do not want to work is eventually translated into employees' behavior patterns which helps the autocratic manager achieve his negative expectations. After all, can anyone honestly be expected to make such a manager a success?

The Organizational Shift

Once there is recognition of the need for an organization to move away from the autocratic management style, supervisory and management skill development takes on a new meaning. As organizations shift from the autocratic management style and concepts, the question of order and control over employees invariably is raised. The way in which rules are to be enforced and discipline applied is a natural, understandable concern in such situations.

Obviously, there must be some form of effective control if chaos is to be avoided. Self-imposed or self-managed control is certainly the ideal way to avoid chaos. Worker groups that have a true participative role have clearly demonstrated their ability to develop a self-controlled environment that is conducive to efficiency and greater productivity. The satisfaction derived from the success in doing this and in having been given recognition for suggestions or improvements in the production process, tends to promote an even greater effort. Where worker groups have been established, they usually set higher goals for themselves and have achieved quality in reaching those goals. Under autocratic management styles where goals are imposed and little recognition is given the worker, this kind of success is not possible.

There is a time and place where the autocratic management style is necessary and can be very effective when properly used. An example is when a sound policy decision is made with which everyone may not agree. Assuming the new policy is sound and has been communicated and explained to the workers, then 100% conformance is a must. Listening and questioning to obtain feedback is vital to obtain an understanding. When a very small percentage of individuals fail to accept the policy, the autocrat is in business. His approach should be to make the policy his policy, communicate his commitment, assume responsibility for the results and simply state: "This is my requirement, it is firm, I will discuss it with you individually; however, if you want to work for me in this department, this is what you must do. Period". Now the temporary autocrat has time to return to his dominate role as a Participative Team Manager. When this process takes place, respect improves, and there is cooperation and commitments with better communications.

49

In situations where employees feel responsible and have a commitment to their employer, their job, and to their work group, tardiness and absenteeism cease to be significant problems. For many years in the United States, the time clock has played the role of manager. When the time clock is punched 10 minutes late, the penalty system is triggered. Such an approach merely adds to the vicious circle of souring work attitudes. On the other hand, in self-managing work groups, the late-arriving employee will probably be motivated to work harder to make up for being late. Group pressure or peer pressure is a very effective motivating force in self-discipline and self-managed work situations.

Think of the time and money that could be saved if all time clocks were put on the scrap heap. Actual time lost due to maintaining tardiness, absenteeism, and attendance records and time spent on disciplinary action could be redirected to more productive activities. These problems have evolved due to failure to develop supervisors and managers.

The Quick Fix

The quick fix has been to build a Human Resource Department which then deals with the symptoms of the problem. American workers (including supervision) have never fully accepted tardiness or absenteeism as a cost factor that reduces productivity and increases costs to the company. Benefit programs often encourage a certain amount of absenteeism. Employees are given warning slips, but it has not been properly communicated as to why their presence and participation is a vital part of the operation. This is another management failure.

Talk about scraping the time clocks and a chill hits the autocratic manager. If you want to cause a coronary, predict that in the near future first line supervisors will be eliminated and the workers will be on a self-management basis. The number of individuals who formerly were supervisors will be reduced and the remaining people will act as assistants, trainers, consultants and resource specialists. This is already taking place in many organizations.

A variety of Job Enrichment Programs have been developed in recent years in order to improve efficiency and productivity. Improved benefits, working conditions and pay advocated in job enrichment have produced job satisfaction which has not as originally intended, caused workers to achieve higher levels of performance. In large measure, it appears that job satisfaction results from higher performance, a sense of being a part of the organization and contributing to productivity. Job Enrichment Programs were never sound and were used as a crutch. These programs have failed because they have not permitted the worker to feel a personal responsibility to reach a goal and develop commitments to higher goals and standards of performance.

Job satisfaction is achieved from high performance with a responsibility to reach a goal, make a commitment, and manage oneself. Managers achieve self-management, direction, and motivation with a high degree of satisfaction through performance. The ineffective, substandard manager lives with stress, anxiety, and fear of being discovered. Successful managers are motivated by achieving goals, and getting and giving recognition for achievement. Are not other employees motivated likewise?

Undoubtedly, not enough attention has been paid to the root cause of worker attitudes and expectations. Negative attitudes and negative expectations produce negative results. There is a great need to move away from the generalization about negative attitudes and negative expectations. In other words, the specific negative attitudes and what an individual believes and feels, needs to be identified and in each case, their causes identified. The causes of negative attitudes are generally generated from management practices, policies, and inadequate leadership in the organizational culture. There is really only one way to change the negative attitudes and expectations in the workplace and that is to change the attitudes of supervisors-managers and the organizational culture. This means returning to the basics.

Goal Setting

Discussions of goals and goal setting in Management Development Programs provide some interesting information. While there may be corporate or plant wide goals, it is rare when supervisors and managers feel that these goals are their goals. Goals are set at the top and are seldom communicated down to the line supervisors, managers or to the workers.

In a meeting with a CEO, the question was asked, "Does your division have a goal or a plan?" The response was positive at the plant manager level; however, nothing had been transmitted below that level. Only the top individuals in the corporation were aware of the goals, but the individuals who were responsible for achieving these goals, had never been informed as to the goals and expectations of the company. The reasons given range from "It is none of their business" to "I didn't consider it important". Corporate goals must be communicated if line goals are to be established and if they are to be meaningful.

First line supervisors and workers seldom have specific job related or personal goals. Also, they have not been informed of the company goals.

When asked to discuss goals, their response includes such comments as, "I do what I'm told, I do the best I can, I put in my eight hours, if I'm not criticized, I guess I'm doing what I ought to be doing". Can you imagine first line supervisors not having a goal or plan? This has to be contributing to the problems of productivity, tardiness, absenteeism and maintaining an inefficient department. Without goals to which people are committed, they can not know where they are going or when they may arrive. The lack of goals contributes to the aimlessness experienced by so many workers, their supervisors and managers. Without goals to which all can readily identify, commitment to improved performance is hardly possible.

We are operating in a culture which discourages creativity, growth and genuine team efforts. A culture which undermines corporate loyalty, fosters shortsightedness, and points the finger of blame. The responsibility for changing productivity problems lies at management's door. We need to change our thinking on what management is all about. Management should develop people to be productive and enjoy themselves in the process.

1. Douglas McGregor, *The Human Side of Enterprise* (New York: McGraw-Hill, 1958).
2. A. H. Maslow, *Motivation and Personality* (New York: Harper & Row, 1954).

6

DELEGATION

The word delegation has different meanings in management depending on individual beliefs, management styles and the organizational culture. Delegation is often mismanaged by assigning unpleasant or minor activities to a subordinate. Genuine delegation involves offering subordinates a challenge with an opportunity to grow and acquire new skills. Delegation is development of people and the organization through participation and improved productivity.

Delegation is often discouraged by our management system especially with middle managers. Ineffective delegation is encouraged by adversarial working relationships, a lack of trust, restrictive job descriptions and subjective performance evaluations.

True delegation means trust and understanding between the parties involved. Delegating is to entrust one's responsibilities and authority with another. A lack of trust is caused by unsound management actions and practices. Ask supervisors-managers how they delegate and what part of their job they delegate. The responses will be varied but the majority will indicate they have never given any thought to the subject. Those that have thought about delegating will indicate they delegate the least liked or more difficult parts of their job. In addition, they often delegate to a selected few "dependable" employees. These employees are individuals that have the skills to perform, are dependable in a crisis and will get the job done. A careful analysis of the delegation procedure will indicate that favoritism or bias is actually involved and some workers are not being given the opportunity to acquire new job knowledge and skills. There are several directions to be taken in delegating responsibilities.

Types of Delegation

Superior to Subordinate—Superior to subordinate is the normal and desired direction in delegating responsibilities. This follows the organizational structure and is intended to have the activities conducted or the decisions made at the level which will be the most cost effective and work flow efficient.

Subordinate to Superior—Subordinate to superior is reverse or upward delegation where the subordinate keeps the boss busy by asking for assistance. Employees become aware of managers that thrive on making all the decisions. For the subordinate, it is an opportunity to help build the superior's ego. In this environment, subordinates learn that it is safer to let the boss do the work. Reverse delegation usually involves decisions and activities which could have been accomplished by the subordinate with some training and proper job instructions.

Reverse delegation can be identified and observed by noting individuals who consistently do the work of their subordinates. Subordinates learn this type of delegation well and are able to keep the boss busy. Reverse delegation is a destructive process with the long-term result being that subordinates are unable to act and think independently. Reverse delegation is also identified as oversupervision.

Horizontal Delegation—Horizontal delegation is the delegation of responsibilities to a fellow employee in a similar or identical position. Some individuals are not good at paperwork or reports, and by way of horizontal delegation, they can transfer their work to peers. A supervisor who dislikes completing reports will attempt to horizontally transfer his shortcomings to an assistant or another supervisor. On the surface, horizontal delegation appears to be an improper practice. However, if this practice improves productivity, it then becomes a sound procedure. Horizontal delegation is a natural method of recognizing and capitalizing on an individual's strengths as long as the individual performing the task is recognized for his performance and the achieved results. When properly handled, horizontal delegation becomes an element in Participative Team Management.

Barriers to Effective Delegation—There are many barriers to effective delegation. Attempts at delegating trivial or distasteful responsibilities will cause the subordinate to feel exploited and possibly withdraw from accepting any future responsibilities beyond what is necessary to survive. Trust and respect were never established or have been destroyed, therefore, the working relationship will remain guarded.

One of the greatest barriers to effective delegation are restrictive job descriptions. Job descriptions typically list the numerous responsibilities a person should perform. The same job description is often used to determine the salary range of the job. It becomes apparent to the individual filling the job that these responsibilities are important. The danger lies in whether these responsibilities are realistic and reflect current organizational goals and objectives.

Performance evaluations are often based on how well the person fulfilled the responsibilities set forth in the job description. It soon becomes apparent to the individual that it is in his best interest to preserve these responsibilities for monetary purposes and job security. Also, the individual working with job description responsibilities will often reject delegation by responding, "It is not in my job description".

Do-Nothing Delegation

Another barrier to effective delegation is the development of adversarial relationships. This begins with a lack of mutual trust. The subordinate rejects delegation and the superior who is lacking in skills and self-confidence will be apprehensive to delegate responsibilities.

Another problem in delegating is when the superior expects the delegated responsibilities to be done exactly as he, the superior, does them. No credit or allowance is given for common sense, creativity, or for the time it takes to learn and acquire the skills necessary to perform the job well. The impatient superior then decides it is easier and quicker to do it himself. The subordinate, with an imposed feeling of inadequacy, will not volunteer a second time.

Delegating responsibility without the necessary authority creates difficulty for the subordinate and increases his chance for failure. The failing subordinate becomes alienated and will be reluctant to accept additional responsibilities in the future.

The "do-nothing" manager delegates by abdication, whereby the subordinates do the job while the boss maintains a low profile, avoids conflicts and opportunities. This often results in the subordinates by-passing their immediate superior and transferring or looking for another job.

There are additional reasons why managers reject delegating:

1. They are unwilling to let go of responsibilities and authority.
2. They fail to see delegation as a means of building team effort.
3. They do not know what should be delegated—ignorance.
4. They are jealous of their better people.
5. Their lack of trust.
6. The fear of taking prudent risks.
7. They fail to develop the subordinates skills.

55

Subordinates reject delegation by failing to see delegation as a means of growing or learning. Guidelines to proper delegation are as follows:

1. Understand the strengths and limitations of each subordinate.
2. Delegate as a part of an employee development plan.
3. Spell out the ground rules, responsibilities and authority.
4. Agree on the expected results—the Standards of Performance.
5. Go from monitoring of the subordinate to self-management.
6. Follow-up and reward performance.

To truly delegate means that we really trust another to do a job. This motivates subordinates to assume greater responsibilities. To achieve this, managers need to start delegating their favorite jobs to subordinates, thereby freeing their time for new and more difficult assignments and activities.

The individuals accepting additional responsibilities and new opportunities should be recognized for their achievement. Failure to recognize and properly reward achievement is irresponsible and destructive behavior. Quite often, all it takes is a simple "Thanks".

Improperly managed attempts at delegation can also result in failure. Frequently, the superior feels he must do the work, thereby leading himself to believe he is indispensable. He then arrogantly states that the employees are lazy and will not take on additional responsibilities.

Delegation should be considered part of the organizational and participative team development. Through additional responsibilities, individuals are given the time and opportunity to acquire new skills and grow as individuals. Managers should start by delegating routine elements of their job and those responsibilities which they know and do well. A skilled manager's time can then be directed to the more difficult and important areas. At the same time, subordinates can acquire new skills, become involved, trusted and respected for their contributions to productivity. Individuals who feel a part of the organization will be more productive.

Delegation of responsibilities is essential in an organization. Regardless of the size of the organization, delegation is a required skill. Delegation forces skilled managers to better utilize their time toward more important tasks and toward new activities and challenges that provide an opportunity for both personal and organizational growth.

7

MEASURING INDIVIDUAL PRODUCTIVITY AND STANDARDS OF PERFORMANCE

The measurement of individual productivity is not new. There are several approaches to measuring productivity, many are simply a method of subjectively measuring results. Individuals and consulting organizations have made a bureaucratic career of developing these programs which essentially measure the likes and dislikes of subordinates.

Two familiar measurement programs are Performance Evaluation and Performance Appraisal. Each program can be effective if properly defined, detailed and implemented to evaluate or appraise measurable results. The term 'appraisal' is usually used to describe an activity of assisting and coaching a subordinate on a continuous basis. Evaluation is usually used to describe a formal measurement of performance for pay or promotion purposes. The terms are used differently by various organizations depending on internal practices.

Measuring Individual Productivity (MIP) is essential if the management system is to be effective and revitalized. An objective MIP program will:

1. Assure that predetermined corporate and organizational goals are achieved.
2. Identify problems and conflicts which hinder productivity improvements.
3. Measure individual job performance.
4. Fairly reward individuals for performance.
5. Identify specific individual development needs.

Many organizations believe they have a program to objectively accomplish the above. Others express the need for an effective system for objective measurement of individual productivity.

Like/Dislike Factors

Organizations that believe they have an effective evaluation program usually have taken one of three approaches. The first approach is where nothing is in writing and quite often the individual being evaluated is unaware of the process. As far as he is concerned, he had never been evaluated. His superior or "someone" does the evaluation and determines the pay raise. The superior can evaluate as he pleases, based on his "like" and "dislike" factors. The percent of pay increase will often reflect his personal feelings. This superior can do as he pleases and as far as he is concerned, he is being fair and objective. More importantly, he likes it this way and will continue with this procedure. The superior likes the power he possesses when he sits in judgement and directly controls an individual's income and future.

A second approach to evaluation is the laundry list of personality traits and work habits such as "cooperation, knowledge, skill, and attitude". The superior checks off each item either as poor, fair, good, or excellent. As with the first approach, it is difficult to be objective and not have the personal like and dislike factors guiding the pen. Typically, no one is rated excellent unless slated for promotion, and no one is rated poor unless targeted for discharge.

Either evaluation approach may involve having the superior meet the subordinate face-to-face. Several possible situations can result from this approach. Often the superior will hand the completed evaluation form to the person who is told to sign it, or they may jointly review each item on the laundry list or in the job description, citing actual recent examples of behavior and activities as perceived by the evaluator.

The typical session may involve Joe the superior calling John, the subordinate into his office. The ensuing discussion may go something like this:

"John, I've called you in so we could go over your performance for the past year. As you know, we do this on an annual basis to determine your pay raise." John indicates that's OK with him. Joe asks John how he feels he has done in the past year. John states, "Fine, I think I've done great. Everything is going well, we are doing the same as before." Joe says, "That's good, I agree with you, I'll give you all good ratings. I can't make them all excellent, although you deserve it, since someone may question it. Is that OK with you John?" John indicates his approval and Joe says, "OK, meet you at 5:00 a.m. on Sunday for fishing." A slight "like" factor is involved with this evaluation.

In an effort to develop an objective Performance Evaluation program and eliminate the subjective "like/dislike" factors as illustrated above, the services of a management consulting firm are engaged. The firm quickly announces they understand the problem and will resolve it. Their approach, to the delight of the Personnel Manager and the autocratic manager, is to develop a massive set of job descriptions. These job descriptions list all the responsibilities and duties in great detail. No one is required to consider actual measurable results achieved as a means of evaluating performance. *Table 7-1* illustrates the shortcomings of a typical job description.

Table 7-1
Job Description

Production Foreman
John A. Doe

Foreman Function:	Responsible for improving operations to increase productivity and reduce operating costs; for production of parts in accordance with the daily work/job schedule; to meet established specifications, routings, methods and labor standards at the lowest cost possible.
Supervision:	Supervises the utilization and productivity of approximately 40 direct and indirect department employees.
Major Responsibilities:	1. Coordinates department operations with other production departments, i.e., Tool Room, Staff Engineering, Maintenance and Quality Control activities in the plant.
	2. Effective utilization and productivity of direct and indirect employees and utilization of productive machines.
	3. Directs set-up of primary, secondary and finish machining including broaching, drilling, boring, turning, deburring operations and surface grinding.
	4. Performs other duties as assigned on Production Duty List.
Responsible For:	1. Plans work orders into production to meet the delivery dates established in accordance with the daily work center schedule that is established by Production Control in accordance with the established routings, standards and methods.
	2. Assigns work to production machine operators

Table 7-1 continued

under your direct supervision to fully utilize manhours and skills on a two-shift basis, and to balance loads among available employees.

3. Selects and loads machine group to obtain the most efficient set-ups and machine program to achieve maximum utilization of equipment, and to meet machine group designation and delivery requirements according to the daily schedule.

4. Frequently monitors work progress to insure that operating delays are minimized, quality standards and production schedules are being met, and that routings and manufacturing methods are being followed.

5. Investigates and identifies production delays resulting from poor material, close tolerance, machine tool malfunction, work programming, etc. Identifies problems and corrective action to be taken.

6. Notifies Plant Superintendent, Production Control, and other foremen waiting for parts of major delays affecting the daily job schedule. Reassigns work and reschedules work to meet other schedule requirements.

7. Participates in method, standards, routing, and machine capability studies conducted in the department.

8. Reviews department manpower and machine utilization, scrap and rework rates, production efficiency, and delivery experience against goals.

9. Recommends installing changes which will improve department efficiency.

10. Identifies poor performance and improvement needs. Plans for improvement are developed with supervisory approval to achieve goals.

11. Prepares reports concerning activities of the department in control of operations and prepara-

Table 7-1 continued

tion of manpower, cost and equipment, and plant forecasts as requested.

12. Interviews and recommends hire of new employees.

13. Solicits requisitions, materials, supplies and tools necessary to the operations; reviews and certifies scrap and rework tickets; approves time cards, and controls other costs within budgeted limits.

14. Identifies training needs in department and develops training plans to improve employee performance with approval from the Superintendent.

15. Reviews performance and progress of employees at regular intervals to ensure expected performance standards are met. Recommendations are made to Personnel as to granting wage increases, retaining or releasing new employees at the end of the probationary period and taking corrective action in cases of consistently poor performance or due to infractions of rules and regulations.

16. Enforces plant regulations and rules, establishes safe operating practices, ensures that employees are wearing required personal protective devices and housekeeping standards are met according to company specifications.

17. Meets with the Plant Superintendent regularly to establish specific departmental and personal improvement goals, reviews progress and develops plans of action to achieve these goals.

18. Reviews and approves production planning, machine loading and work assignment made to deburrers and production machine operators by the Assistant Foreman when assigned to the department.

19. Requests assistance from Tool Design, Quality Control, Tool Room, Maintenance and Industrial Engineering to correct routing, methods, programming standards and major machine or tooling

Table 7-1 continued

malfunctions and breakdowns.
20. Notifies shop employees of any changes in their wage or job status. Handles personnel problems in the department and complaints of employees. Consults with Personnel and with the Plant Superintendent on serious or major personnel problems before taking appropriate action.

The Objective Evaluation

A year later with the new job description in place, it is time for Joe to do John's first "objective" Performance Evaluation. Joe calls John into his office and the same discussion of a year ago ensues. The "like" factor is still involved even with the new job description. It is not possible for the superior to be totally objective. Nothing has changed, Joe the superior can still do as he pleases. Joe can still perform a subjective evaluation based on his "like" and "dislike" factor.

Another hypothetical example demonstrates how the "dislike" factor can enter into another person's (Hank's) evaluation based on a job description that is identical to John's. Joe the superior calls Hank into his office for his Performance Evaluation. The conversation may go something like this:

"Hank, it's that time of year for your Performance Evaluation which determines your pay raise. Hank, how do you feel you've done in the past year?" Hank states, "Fine boss, everything has gone well, there have been a few problems, but everything turned out well." Joe says, "Hank, that's not the way I see it. Going through your job description" (which more than likely Hank has never seen), "it says you have a responsibility for quality." Hank replies by stating, "That's right boss and I reduced rejects from 7% to 5 ½% which is good." Joe says, "That's not the way I see it Hank, I wanted rejects reduced to 3%." Hank states he did not know this and Joe then tells him he should have.

Joe then asks Hank about his control over absenteeism. Hank proudly responds by reporting that it has been reduced by 20%. Joe retorts, "Hank, if I recall correctly, last year in your evaluation I told you I wanted absenteeism reduced by 50%." Hank responds by stating that this is not how he remembers it. Hank now perceives Joe as saying, I am the boss, I can do as I please—I can rate you as I wish, I can do with you as I please. If there is any pay raise, it will be minimal. Essentially, the only difference that exists between John and Hank's evaluation of their job performance lies in Joe's like or dislike of the individual.

Hank's only recourse is to up-date his resume; however, because of his many years of service with the company, he will probably go back to his department, keep a low profile and try to survive until retirement. A few more evaluations like this and he will be retired on the job.

Efforts have been made to eliminate the like/dislike factor by giving everyone the same percentage pay increase. The outstanding performer receives the same as the substandard-incompetent performer. At that point, the traditional Performance Evaluation programs can be described as failures.

All the nice forms with the laundry list of traits and the impressive job descriptions are more destructive than helpful because they do not seek a common ground of performance standards. How do the job descriptions actually contribute to achieve the objectives and purpose of a Performance Evaluation? They contribute nothing! Recall the objectives:

1. Assure that predetermined corporate and organizational goals are achieved.
2. Identify problems and conflicts which hinder improving productivity.
3. Measure individual job performance.
4. Fairly reward individuals for performance.
5. Identify individual development and training needs.

Senior executives and certain middle managers, depending on their level and responsibilities, should be measured against agreed upon goals and objectives. These are the individuals who should be concentrating on the vital activities that are important to the company instead of being tied down to a long list of responsibilities. Rather, these individuals are expected to set the tone and bring about change. This requires considerable freedom and time for creativity. The MIP for this group requires that specific goals and/or objectives be in writing with a completion date. The assumption is made that the executive at this level will take care of his other responsibilities by doing them himself or through proper delegation.

This assumption cannot be made with entry level management involving first line supervisors, staff and clerical-support personnel. Experience with support personnel who have been involved in an MBO program has shown that each individual concentrated on two or three objectives to the neglect of their total job.

In order to prevent the neglect of certain responsibilities and have an

63

effective measurement of individual productivity, the Standards of Performance are used for certain middle managers, all first line supervisors, staff and clerical personnel as the third approach to evaluation.

Standards of Performance

The Standards of Performance describe the expected results in terms of the conditions that will exist for each individual's responsibilities when acceptable productivity is achieved.

The Standards of Performance approach to achieve results is not new. This approach has been developed, implemented, and is being used on a continuous basis in many organizations. We have been developing and installing this approach in organizations for the past 10 years.

The Standards of Performance is an approach which needs to be defined, understood and accepted if an organization is to be productive and grow. Every job has certain responsibilities and functions which, if carried out, will produce results which can be objectively measured.

The intent of the Standards of Performance is to ensure that achievable goals are set and accomplished to improve productivity. For these goals to be met, each individual must define his job in terms of meeting responsibilities and carrying out assigned activities. This means that there must be a perfect match between the job responsibilities and the person. There are many possible mismatches. The impact of two mismatches is illustrated in *Figure 7-2*.

Manager A is a good manager and he is doing his job well. He is effectively fulfilling all his responsibilities, and providing these job responsibilities are adequate and correct, he will reach his goals.

Manager B is a new manager and is inexperienced, lacks the basic skills, is unsure of himself, and does not know or is just not doing his total job. His Performance and Development Gap is illustrated by an "X".

Manager C is an old timer who has been doing his job the same way for 30 years. He receives regular increases in pay and there is no need to change. He has never done his total job. The Performance and Development Gap is represented by a "Y". Manager C always looks busy because he is doing many activities which are not part of his job. Some of his activities as represented by "Z", are a waste of time and energy since they need not be done. Manager C's superior is unaware of his wasteful activites.

The question is, If Manager B and C are not doing their job as represented by "X" and "Y", who is doing their job? Keep in mind that if the Vice President of Manufacturing is to achieve his objectives, either he or Manager A must do the job. Unfortunately, by the Vice President of

Manufacturing doing part of Manager's B and C's job, B and C are delegating upward which makes the Vice President of Manufacturing feel important and keeps him busy. Manager A, being effective and doing his total job, will eventually leave for another job when he realizes that B and C earn the same money and receive the same raises and recognition.

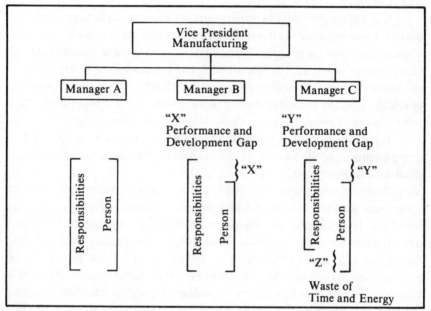

*Figure 7-2.** Mismatched Job Responsibilities
* Originator of this figure is unknown.

The Standards of Performance are designed to identify and eliminate performance gaps and to ensure that managers, supervisors and support personnel are aware of the following:

1. What is supposed to be done and what their responsibilities are.
2. What the scope and degree of each responsibility will be.
3. How well he is expected to perform and the standard he is expected to meet.
4. How well he is actually performing—the measurement of results.

Initiating the Standards

The Standards of Performance development process is initiated by having each individual list their responsibilities in writing as they see them. It should be pointed out that it can be a very difficult and painful process for a line supervisor to put his responsibilities in writing. Our experience is that few have ever given it any thought. The responsibilities as initially developed by line supervisors, range from a statement such as: "Get to work on time, check the time cards and make sure everyone is busy" to a fairly detailed list of responsibilities.

In development sessions, supervisors are asked to outline their responsibilities. Their response is almost instantaneous and many times quite vague. Typical responses range from: "I don't know", and "no one ever told me", to "they change everyday". When asked when and how their performance is evaluated, the majority will respond that they have never had a performance evaluation. In our Developmental program with first line supervisors, 80% indicated they have never had a Performance Evaluation.

John Doe's draft of his responsibilities as he sees them are used to demonstrate the Standards of Performance Development Process as illustrated in *Figure 7-3*.

Once responsibilities are listed, the individual's immediate superior must meet with the employee and agree on the responsibilities. There are usually a few surprises at this point. Usually, the individual has listed activities his superior was unaware he was doing. The superior does not want him using his time and energy on activities that do not contribute to productivity. As a result, some responsibilities are often omitted. Seldom is there any resemblance between the individual's formal job description and his actual responsibilities. The key at this point is to find out how the individual perceives his job and what he is actually doing.

In one organization, management was shocked to discover they had 23 foreman functioning as purchasing agents. Each foreman was dealing directly with vendors and purchasing his own supplies. As a consequence, the foremen's time was spent taking calls from vendors, listening to vendors and generally neglecting their important duties involving quality and production. The actual purchasing agent was a paper shuffler. It goes without saying that some dramatic changes took place.

Once there is agreement on the job responsibilities, the individual is then asked to develop a standard for each responsibility. Putting a standard in writing requires an employee to think in terms of results versus activities. To many this is a new experience. The Standard is defined as follows: "The Standard is a written statement of the conditions which will exist when a specific responsibility is well done and acceptable to the individual's

Standards of performance

Name   John A. Doe
Job title   Production Foreman
Period

Responsibility	Standard	Results
1) Coordinates work with Production Control to meet production schedule.		
2) Assign work to machines on 2 shift basis.		
3) Check process of work for delays and quality.		
4) Communicate with my supervisors and subordinates on any major delay.		
5) Contact supporting services for needed assistance to make quality parts.		
6) Review manufacturing process for improvement.		
7) Coordinates training of new employees and make periodic review of process.		
8) Handle complaints within the department.		

Figure 7-3. Standards of Performance Development Process

67

immediate superior." The Standard must be:

1. In writing;
2. Measurable;
3. Attainable and,
4. Agreed on between the subordinate and superior.

The Standard may be in negative or positive terms. See *Figure 7-4* for John Doe's initial draft of his Standards of Performance prior to agreement with his superior. *Figure 7-5* illustrates the Standards of Performance following agreement with his superior.

The Standards of Performance cover an individual's total job. They are his total job responsibilities with written, measurable results to be achieved. Initially, there will be some Standards which are not in measurable terms. The question the superior must constantly ask is, "How do you want to be measured in this area?" and "How will I know when you are doing this responsibility well?"

The Standards of Performance covering the individual's total basic job must be in existence prior to considering MBO. The exception is with certain middle managers and all of top management where MBO's can be effective when properly implemented.

Once the Standards of Performance are completed, there should be a quarterly Performance Evaluation, not for monetary purposes but to assist the subordinate in achieving results and self-development, and if necessary, to adjust the Standards so they are reasonable and attainable. It takes about three to four Performance Evaluations before the Standards of Performance will accurately reflect the true picture.

When a subordinate fails to meet an agreed upon Standard, either the Standard was too high, there were conditions or factors beyond his control, or he simply did not perform. The individual may need to develop a specific area of his supervisory and management skills. The individual may have trouble meeting his Standard on controlling rejects. The superior must then work with the individual to assist and identify the cause. At this point, the individual may need assistance on how to give proper job instructions or improve his communications skills.

Identifying Training Needs

Organizations spend money on programs designed to determine training needs. Usually the determination is that everyone needs training in communications. This is usually false. Some may need training in communications, but not all. One supervisor may have problems communicating, which

Standards of performance

Name John A. Doe
Job title Production Foreman
Period

Responsibility	Standard	Results
1) Coordinates work with Production Control to meet production schedule.	1) Usually meet stated finish date given to Production Control.	
2) Assign work to machines on 2 shift basis.	2) Skills of operators are utilized to maximum output.	
3) Check process of work for delays and quality.	3) Constantly check on process and quality of work being done.	
4) Communicate with my supervisors and subordinates on any major delay.	4) Proper people informed about any delay or improvement of schedule.	
5) Contact supporting services for needed assistance to make quality parts.	5) Work with Industrial Engineering and Inspection and Tool Design to improve part quality.	
6) Review manufacturing process for improvement.	6) Recommend process changes to better utilize equipment.	
7) Coordinates training of new employees and make periodic review of process.	7) Check on progress of training on a regular basis.	
8) Handle complaints within the department.	8) Few complaints.	

Figure 7-4. Initial Draft of the Standards of Performance

Standards of performance

Responsibility

1) Coordinates work with Production Control to meet production schedule.

2) Assign work to machines on 2 shift basis.

3) Check process of work for delays and quality.

Standard

1) Will meet delivery dates in accordance with established routings, methods and standards 95% on time with remaining 5% being due to circumstances beyond my control. No legitimate complaints from Production Control.

2) Manhours and skills will be fully (100% of time) utilized to balance loads among available employees. No legitimate complaints from employees, my superior or other department supervisors.

3) Monitor progress of work to insure that operating delays are minimized and quality standards are being met. This will be done on a hourly basis with the reduction in delays improved by 20% and the quality improved 25% within the next three months.

Results

4) Communicate with my supervisors and subordinates on any major delay.	4) Over next three months will improve my communication 80% with no legitimate complaints.
5) Contact supporting services for needed assistance to make quality parts.	5) An immediate request will be made to supporting services for assistance to correct routing methods, programming standards and major machine or tooling malfunctions and breakdowns. No complaints from my superiors as to not doing this.
6) Review manufacturing process for improvement.	6) Will insure efficient and economical operation. Will reduce scrap and rework by 20% within next three months and downtime by 20%.
7) Coordinates training of new employees and make periodic review of process.	7) All new employees will be trained by proper job instructions and monitored as needed. No damage to product, equipment or facility due to no or improper training.
8) Handle complaints within the department.	8) There are few complaints from my employees, would like to reduce them to zero complaints.

Figure 7-5. Standards of Performance Following Agreement with Superior

71

does not mean all supervisors need a course in communications. Using the Standards of Performance with a quarterly evaluation is the most ideal, reliable and practical method of identifying training and development needs. If an individual is unable to meet his Standard, his supervisor is responsible for ensuring that the subordinate's Development Gap is corrected through additional coaching, training and development. This eliminates guesswork and avoids expensive analysis to determine development needs.

The "Results" column (as illustrated in *Figure 7-5*) is for noting the results achieved and the areas where the supervisor needs assistance.

Do the Standards of Performance meet the criteria for an objective performance evaluation? An objective MIP will accomplish the following:

1. Assure that predetermined corporate and organizational goals are achieved.
2. Identify problems and conflicts which hinder improving productivity.
3. Measure individual job performance.
4. Fairly reward individuals for performance.
5. Identify specific individual development and training needs.

Individual's benefit from the Standards of Performance because they:

1. Know their responsibilities.
2. Know how well they must perform in their job.
3. Understand the scope and degree of their responsibilities.
4. Are permitted to establish their priorities and plan to achieve their goals.
5. Know how their performance will be measured.
6. Show where they need to improve.
7. Are aware that two levels of management above their supervisor will review their Standards of Performance.

The Standards of Performance provide an objective method of measuring performance. Most importantly, the Standards provide a method of identifying and eliminating performance gaps. The Standards of Performance play a major role in revitalizing and developing management and in improving productivity.

8

COMMUNICATIONS

Good communication practices are one of the greatest enhancements to improving productivity. The importance of communications in the workplace has been stressed and restressed. No one will argue with the fact than an individual must be able to communicate well to be an effective manager.

There are many textbooks, courses, and numerous seminars and workshops on the subject of effective communications. In spite of this and with all the publications and specialists in the field, inadequate and ineffective communications remain a problem. In the hundreds of development programs we have conducted with thousands of managers, communication is always identified as the number one problem in managing. This chapter is directed at determining how a manager can identify and resolve the problems and barriers to effective communications.

The Basic Principles

The basic principles of effective communication are well-known. The basis for good communication is an understanding of the principles and practices involved in the communication process. Quite often individuals feel they are communicating when they give instructions. This will be the same individual who does not understand why subordinates do not follow instructions. Managers often state: "I tell them what to do again and again and they still do it wrong". Subordinates, superiors, and fellow managers are blamed for being poor communicators. It is always the other person who has a problem communicating.

People who blame others for being poor communicators do not realize that communication is a two-way process. By telling someone what to do or giving them instructions, does not necessarily mean that the message has been effectively communicated. Feedback that the message and the instructions have been received and are understood is essential.

Listening

The communication process requires practiced listening skills by both the sender and the receiver.

A good listening skill exercise is to take a group of 20 managers, divide them into four teams, give each team a case study to analyze, and three case questions to respond to as a team. Each team is given a different situation regarding the problem and the facts. Each team will "assume" they all have the identical case. After each team has agreed on their responses to the questions, have them discuss and justify their responses as a group of twenty. Our experience is that after the first clue has been given, the groups continue their discussions as if they were discussing the same case. Our record-holding group went 28 minutes "assuming" they were discussing the same case.

This same practice holds true with meetings. Meetings have been rightly identified as consuming a high percentage of a manager's time and also as the greatest time waster.

Individuals attending a meeting are often ill-prepared for reasons of lack of an advance agenda or poor preparation on the part of the person conducting the meeting. Often each individual has a different perspective, goal and/or personal interest for attending the meeting. The meeting concludes with the person conducting the meeting often obtaining what he wants, while individual's will leave the meeting and comment "What was that all about" or "I don't agree with the conclusion".

Listening is a skill which too few have perfected. Poor listening skills are a major problem in communication. Ideas, innovations, and creativity are often missed when we do not listen or question skillfully. New ideas, problems and opportunities are often initiated from the lower ranks.

The problem in listening arises from the fact that most individuals think about four times as fast as the average person speaks. Therefore, the listener has three-quarters of a minute of spare thinking time for each listening minute. The extra time is often used to think about personal affairs, concerns, and subjects unrelated to what the speaker is saying. Listening is essential, none of us learn anything while we are talking.

Questioning

Another major element for effective communication is the development of good questioning skills. The ability to ask the proper type of questions in a manner that obtains all the facts and then results in a complete understanding between the parties involved, is essential for sound management actions and decisions. There is a tendency after a problem and solution have been presented for the presentor to state, "That is the problem and the solutions, are there any questions?" If communications are not open within an organization, then the discussion or meeting will probably be over. The individual presenting the problem and solution can avoid this by using a direct question approach to each individual by name. This forces a response to the problem, and a discussion of the advantages, disadvantages, and alternatives to the problem.

Principles for effective communication are available, have been tried, tested, and proven. In spite of this, communication remains a major problem to improving productivity in the workplace.

The underlying causes of poor communications have not been fully identified and are not fully understood. As a consequence, the corrective effort is usually a superficial treatment of the symptoms. Communication is an innate, basic instinct, although effective communication skills do not come naturally. Effective communication skills are learned through practice and application.

The real problem with effective communications is two-fold. That is, employees bring various cultural backgrounds into an organization, in addition to the established behavior patterns that are already in existence within an organization. The problem in industry is like a two-sided coin. Both sides, which are opposite yet connected, are essential to the whole. Both aspects must be identified and defined if corrective measures are to be taken and managers are to learn to communicate more effectively.

The barriers to effective communications involve five interrelated but independent areas. They are:

1. Recognized Barriers (of race, religion, sex, etc.).
2. Cultural Barriers.
3. Organizational Barriers.
4. Leadership-Management Styles.
5. Credibility Discounters.

Recognized Barriers

The barriers which interfer with normal communications have been identified as race, religion, sex, education, terminology, slang, language, money status, and age. These barriers are all man-made and continue to exist only when an individual wants to obstruct effective communications. Barriers

75

to effective communications can be readily identified, understood and eliminated with sound leadership.

Cultural Barriers

Today we hear about the black culture, the hispanic culture, the southern culture and many more. Beliefs and customs of various ethnic groups, nationalities, and religious groups determine their individual practices and behavior. One group will perceive another group as inferior or superior, and possessing certain customs which are to them, foreign. These perceptions also include the man-made barriers of race, religion, sex, etc. Cultural or "learned" behavior is often interpreted as foreign or unfamiliar, and thus becomes a barrier to effective communications.

Individual cultural barriers interfers with the communication process only when one permits it to become a barrier. The barrier is there and will remain in place since each individual naturally reflects his or her beliefs based on their own individual culture.

The challenge then becomes one of recognition and acceptance of people as individuals who have a right to their cultural beliefs. It is essential for people to be empathetic toward those who have different cultural beliefs, and not to be indifferent or to have a patronizing attitude. Only then can people develop the ability to relate to others so that all become more open and receptive to effective communication.

There are, of course, situations where cultural beliefs and behavioral patterns interfere with sound, effective management practices. Although each individual is entitled to his beliefs, behavior which is detrimental to an organization can not be condoned. Each organization has established guidelines and policies which must apply to all. This means that guidelines for acceptable behavior must be identified and understood. This approach may sound like management by constraint. This is not constraint, rather, it is understanding an individual's beliefs and why this individual believes differently than you. Once a manager understands and accepts the right of an individual to be different, the manager can then capitalize on an individual's creativity to make the best decisions and obtain the best solutions to his problems.

The question then is how to modify behavior that is nonproductive or detrimental to a group of workers and to the organization as a whole. Behavior patterns are determined by beliefs. Beliefs concerning acceptable behavior in the work place can be changed through effective communications, by providing guidance through individual coaching and organization-wide management skill development. It now becomes essential to have supervisors and managers who are qualified in their positions.

Organizational Barriers

The organizational culture creates major communication barriers. These barriers are also man-made, and are created at the top of an organization. The organizational culture is defined as: "The combined leadership-management styles, practices, and attitudes which determine the level and quality of activities, the degree of creativity and motivation, and the working environment".

Within an organizational culture, there is often a departmental and a work group culture which affects communications. This also explains the differences that exist from one group to another, from one department to another, and from one organization to another.

The traditional manager, the autocrat, creates communication barriers by authoritarian actions, superior attitudes, and refusal to listen to subordinates. By suppressing feedback, incentives are destroyed and resistance is created. As a result, growth of employees and the organization becomes severly restricted.

Why do we have communication problems when effective communication techniques have been well-known for some time? The answer is that organizational cultures are not structured to provide an open, candid, receptive climate for effective communication to exist. Insecurity, lack of trust, and simple ignorance prevents changing toward the development of a sound organizational culture which is necessary to establishing effective communications.

The various communication situations that exist within an organization can be identified and grouped as follows:

1. An individual's failure to acquire the basic knowledge necessary to understand a problem. Possibly the individual sees no need to acquire this knowledge, has never been exposed to the knowledge areas necessary to obtain this information, has not had the opportunity to obtain this information, or just doesn't know what is happening. This also includes the individual who thinks he knows it all.

   Ignorance is one of the easiest areas to correct because once the need is identified, people will learn when proper leadership, direction and developmental opportunities are provided.

2. An individual who acquires the knowledge necessary to understand

the problem, but never develops any skills to deal with the problem. This is caused by a combination of ignorance, insecurity, lack of trust, and fear of change. Failure to develop these skills can be and usually is imposed from above. This failure is caused by a dominating organizational culture.

Knowledge alone is of little value without the skill to use it effectively. Skills are not acquired without application of daily on-the-job activities.

3. An individual acquires the skills necessary to understand a problem and can be an effective communicator under certain circumstances. This individual can communicate effectively under normal circumstances, but under pressure will fold or decide to retreat and remain silent, compromise, or use defensive techniques. The dominant management style of superiors will determine an individual's approach to communications. The climate can easily become one of fear, where an individual sees nothing, hears nothing, and speaks no more.

4. The fourth group consists of people who understand the culture, the organizational climate, management styles and practices, and are able to deal with the situation through empathy and appealing to what motivates the individual. These people not only have the communications skills but also the essential participative team management skills to seek and obtain the best decisions, the best solutions, and the most productive activities. Their individual interests are subordinated to the interest of the organization.

Leadership-Management Styles

Leadership-management styles are learned according to an individual's beliefs and are directly related to an individual's culture and to the organizational culture. Leadership-management styles have been well-defined. Every leader-manager has a different style of communicating. Identifying and understanding a particular style is basic to communicating with an individual. Without this understanding, two individuals that appear to be communicating, may in fact, be failing to agree on their goals and the methods used to achieve them.

In one of our Presupervisory Training Programs, each individual was asked to identify a problem which, if corrected, would improve their job and save the company money. Out of a group of 20 individuals, six of them identified a waste problem. Historically, their company had an accountable

$500,000 annual inventory loss. Six employees working independently, identified the problem as spillage and scraping of good parts at two specific points in the assembly operation. The company made a few simple modifications (which cost less than $100) and recovered and recycled the lost parts. Within two months, the company was showing $40,000 per month in recovered material. The employees who identified the problem worked for an autocratic who openly stated that he did not have time to listen to his employees, nor did he believe his employees knew anything. These employees had always known about the problem but were suppressed into malicious obedience by doing as they were told even though they knew it was wrong.

Executives and plant managers need to visit the plant and break down the communication barriers by talking directly with the workers. This is a tremendous motivational technique both for the workers and managers. Thomas J. Peters and Robert H. Waterman Jr. in their book, *In Search of Excellence* refers to Ed Carlson, Chairman of United Airlines Inc. who labeled this technique "Visible Management" and "MBWA—Management by Walking About". Hewlett Packard (HP) treats MBWA ("Management By Wandering Around") as "a major tenant of all importance to the (HP) way".[1]

Executives and managers who spend time in the work areas are there to observe and listen to the employees, not to give orders or to usurp anyone's authority. These executives and managers should set the example by finding out what employees are thinking and obtain their suggestions. When the first and middle line managers realize what is happening, they will follow the example and the barriers and buffer zones will start to disappear.

In many organizations CEO's are isolated at the top. They are surrounded by individuals who are more concerned with their own track record than with giving the boss accurate information. They seldom see the shop floor. CEO's should spend 25% of their time on the shop floor. The advantages a CEO will learn are problems, conflicts and opportunities he simply can't find out any other way. More importantly, the employees are motivated. They'll feel more a part of the organization.

The practice of spending time on the floor is difficult for some. It requires a commitment. Maintaining a personal time log complete with observations is helpful until this practice becomes a way of managing.

Credibility Discounters

Verbal credibility discounters include terms such as "poor attitude", "biased", "too controversial", "simplistic", "shallow" and "superficial". There are times when these terms are appropriate. Quite often, however, these terms are used as a devise to discredit the speaker, limit, or cut off the discussion.

These terms can be used in a positive manner if there is agreement on what the term means, and constructive alternatives to these terms are offered. Labeling an individual as having a "poor attitude" merely means that you do not like that person's beliefs since his beliefs are different than yours. The term "biased" is essentially used in the same manner; in addition, this term also implies a lack of objectivity.

"Too controversial" is a term used to dispute a new idea someone is attempting to communicate, when there is disagreement on a particular subject, or when challenging a concept. The individual using the term usually is saying that he disagrees with the statement, idea, or subject being communicated, therefore, we should not listen to what is being said. Quite often the most creative, imaginative people have been referred to as controversial.

"Too simplistic", "shallow", and "superficial", are also terms often used to express disagreement. The phrase, "I believe there is much more to it" is usually used in conjunction with these terms. These terms can be appropriately used if a constructive opinion has been based on in-depth thinking. However, the very use of these terms have a tendency to put an individual on the defensive. When these terms are directed at an individual, his only response is to ask what the communicator means by the term used, and then determine what his alternatives are. Verbal credibility discounters can be used in a positive sense; however, they are often used in a negative manner to limit discussions.

Directing Communications

A great deal of time is spent dealing with which way to direct communications. Normally, communications is either upward or downward. The president complains that very little of his communication filters down to the worker. The worker complains that very few of his problems and complaints reach the president. Both are correct. Neither can be ignored, however, there should also be concern for horizontal communications. Very little emphasis is placed in this area. Yet, the product or service moves from department to department on a horizontal basis. Unfortunately, the emphasis on communication is either up and/or down. Emphasis on the communication process should be with the flow of the product, service or knowledge areas within an organization.

The publication, *Organization for Manufacturing* reports on the findings of three experts. Harold J. Leavitt writing in *Managerial Psychology* states:

"...the diminishing role of classic authority in the design of organization structure. Traditional organization is influenced by the military view of authority, but modern organization practice has shown that control can be maintained with much less use of this type of authority. The authority role is being replaced by the roles of communications and coordination, and organizational structures are reflecting this change in thinking. Organizing around work flow to facilitate communication and coordination is antagonistic to the traditional view of organizing around lines of authority.

"Horizontal communication—disregarding hierarchial lines of authority—is more and more prevalent in our organizations. A dramatic example of this is presented by Melville Dalton (*Men Who Manage*) in his report of his study of an industrial firm which he gives the fictional title of Milo Fractionating Center. Dalton shows two organizational charts for Milo—one based on formal authority relationships and one based on communication and informal influence. The two charts bear almost no resemblance to each another.

"Likert (*New Patterns of Management*) introduces a means of horizontal communication and coordination in his "linking-pin" concept, whereby each component is linked to the total organization by means of an overlapping structure."[2]

The simple creation of an add-on organization to coordinate communications is not cost effective or necessary. The answer is in the organizational structure itself, to evaluate the work flow, communications, and adjust activities to this reality.

Nonverbal Communication

Nonverbal communication accounts for 60-65% of our communications. Nonverbal communication is expressed through our facial expressions, eye contact, dress, posture, tone of voice, appearance and physical characteristics. Individuals respond stronger to the nonverbal message than to the verbal message. The nonverbal message actually reflects our beliefs and attitudes toward situations and people we deal with.

Our individual attitudes, beliefs and true feelings are reflected in our total communications. Our like or dislike toward others is usually communicated nonverbally. People who are becoming or who are aware of the importance of nonverbal communications have responded that they conceal the fact that they dislike an individual. The person believes he can treat everyone equally and with the same objectivity, including the individual he likes and someone he may dislike. Unless he is a skilled actor, this is impossible for the average person. As a result, a lack of trust develops. The eyes communicate our true feelings toward an individual. The eyes do not lie.

The individual interested in improving personal communications skills needs to develop the ability and skill in understanding the nonverbal, unspoken message. This is often more important than mastering the language skills. A successful sales person has the skill to determine what the perspective buyer is thinking through nonverbal messages. He can then address the buyer's questions and counter any resistance.

Successful managers automatically read people's nonverbal messages. He is then able to create trust through understanding and empathy. The person unskilled in nonverbal communications relies on telling individuals what to do through the use of authority. People who have developed mutual trust are communicating the same message verbally and nonverbally.

Since nonverbal communications accounts for a high percentage of the communication process, managers need the skills to observe, listen and question. A conference leader or an individual conducting a meeting relies on observing the nonverbal messages and reacting accordingly.

The barriers and problems in communicating are often designed as a screen to disguise weakness. It is a failure to understand, with prejudices, biases, likes and dislikes retarding the growth of individuals and the organization. It is a skilled ignorance, where we can pretend there are no problems. Receptivity to change is superficial with outward verbal concern, and pretending to communicate with a contradictory nonverbal message.

1. Thomas J. Peters and Robert H. Waterman Jr., *In Search of Excellence* (New York: Harper & Row, 1982) p. 122.
2. *Managerial Psychology*, 1964; *Men Who Manage*, 1959; *New Patterns of Management*, 1961, quoted in *Organization for Management* (Dearborn, Michigan: Society of Manufacturing Engineers, 1970), pp. 88-89.

9

MOTIVATION

During a seminar on motivation, a conference leader challenged a group of managers with some interesting results. In previous sessions, the leader defined motivation and discussed the various principles and techniques of motivating. He had listed and discussed people's basic needs and drives using the textbook approach on motivational theory. In the process, he established traditional guidelines and principles in the handling of employees.[1]

The challenge posed to the group of manager's was for each individual to determine each subordinate's primary drive and then appeal to it. In other words, motivate the individual to improve performance. In the following session, the managers discussed what they had done individually in attempting to determine the drives of their employees.

This session was anything but a success. The conference leader took the drives for security, money and recognition and asked the managers to tell him how they would use each drive to appeal to employees. Some suggestions and examples were offered as to how one should proceed. In fact, the managers were merely repeating the techniques outlined in the previous session by the conference leader.

One longtime manager, recognized as being very effective, questioned the need and drive approach. He went on to explain that in his opinion, you, the manager, motivate people based on the person you are, your knowledge, your skill and attitude toward your job, your employees, and the company. Respect was also considered important; however, the major factor was the total manager as a person.

It is possible that the popular emphasis on how to motivate should actually and more properly be directed toward development of the individual on how to effectively manage and be a motivator. It is necessary that the subject of motivation be put in better perspective.

Problems in Motivation

Many of the motivational techniques being proposed to industry indicate that motivation is the most misdirected and misunderstood area in the management field. Because of the preoccupation with motivation, there are individuals spending days conducting courses and seminars to train key personnel on the basic textbook principles involved in motivation, what it is, and how to create and use it. Supervisors and managers are continuously being told to get out there and motivate their employees to be more responsible and productive.

The approaches commonly presented consist of textbook theories and promotional campaigns on how to appeal to employees. The promotional approaches advocated usually involve development or purchase of a packaged campaign consisting of posters, films, medals, premium stamps, and awards which are supposed to appeal to and motivate the masses. The theory approach usually involves a training session to determine the needs and drives of employees as outlined by Maslow in 1954.[2] Herzberg followed in 1959 with his Specific Theory of Motivation.[3]

One major flaw in Herzberg's study was that the examination of events, research and investigation was with engineers and accountants. These people are more or less considered to be removed from plant activities. There is a question whether his findings would apply to the skilled, semiskilled, and unskilled employees, as well as the supervisors and managers that are essential to the organization. There are many varied approaches to motivation being used in industry. The efforts of supervisory and management personnel involved in training-type programs are usually wasted with poor results.

A statement often heard is, "I would consider it an accomplishment if you can show me how to motivate those guys out there". Usually the individual making the statement has already attempted either the textbook technique or promotional campaigns and still has a poor or mediocre work force. These work forces are reluctantly doing the job required to exist, but are doing no more than is absolutely necessary.

It is necessary to recognize that a majority of supervisors and managers have been promoted from the ranks and are seldom provided the benefit of professional training. It's the old story—on Friday, a machine operator, on Monday, a manager, with the responsibility to direct, plan, control, schedule and motivate employees to produce. This may sound easy; however, without proper guidance, training and development, the new manager's effectiveness and performance will in itself, soon be the subject of discussion. Rather than having the ability to successfully develop the inner necessity or drive in employees to excel, the manager is forced into pushing employees in order to survive, which only aggravates the situation.

At this point, the problem of the employee's poor attitude and low level of productivity is passed on to the Human Resource Department. The standard approach to motivating employees is to decide on one of several courses of action:

1. Do nothing.
2. Develop a motivation campaign appealing directly to the employees.
3. Develop a training program based on motivation.

The problems with motivation needs to be put in proper perspective so managers will understand how to create the climate necessary to encourage employees to voluntarily strive for excellence in their jobs and in themselves. Until this is accomplished, millions of dollars will be wasted every year on superficial programs and gimmicks.

In discussing this subject, it is necessary to review the motivational means or techniques that are frequently presented to managers as the best solution.

Do Nothing

The "Do Nothing" approach usually results when management is looking for the "time" to do something. Sometimes this may be the best approach—especially if negative results of a poor approach can be avoided.

Motivational Campaigns

The second approach is to develop or purchase a "canned" promotional campaign to appeal to one and all. This is a dream program which is aimed directly at the employees. Once the decision is made to purchase such a campaign, the manager feels as if he has been relieved of this particular responsibility. The ineffective first line supervisors can go back to doing what they do best—operate their old machine.

There is a growing market for canned training programs consisting of films, manuals and cassets. Unfortunately, they are of limited value when used as the program rather than as a tool for motivation. Approximately 85% effectiveness is determined by the training or conference leader's skill in presenting and conducting the program. In addition, a canned program usually does not properly address internal problems, conflicts and the organization's goals. Unless an individual is self-motivated and on a self-development program, a canned program by itself is a waste of development funds.

The manager's role in motivation is usually ignored as the Staff Human Resource Committee develops and implements the campaign consisting of slogans, posters, medals and awards. These are all designed to motivate the employees. The manager's responsibility has now been usurped by staff specialists.

The manager may soon say, "Why should I worry about it, it is the expert's program and responsibility to motivate employees". The manager cannot effectively use good management practices when a major part of his responsibilities have been displaced.

This problem is supposedly avoided by getting the manager and some of the employees to participate in the development and implementation of the program. Results can be obtained by such promotional programs, but they will be of short duration. The very fact that someone in management demonstrates some concern or interest for the employees will provide some short-term results. This was demonstrated in the Hawthorn Studies.[4]

There are definite negative aspects of such promotional campaigns. First of all, employee interest cannot be maintained month after month. After a time they are likely to "tune out" and become completely unaware of the message.

The campaign must have winners so a few are singled out for special recognition. The rest being losers may resent this, in fact, they may ridicule the recognition bestowed on the selected few. It is also possible for employees to resent such a campaign and consider it an insult to their intelligence. It is possible that the entire program will be disregarded by all but the few singled out for recognition. Ironically, any recognition was probably due long before the campaign started.

The most important factor is that such campaigns fail to get at the heart of employee dissatisfaction. Once the campaign runs out, there is also the possibility that the employees will become hardened to future appeals. Therefore, the next campaign must top the prior ones and be more interesting and entertaining. The fact is, this approach is not good management. It is management with gimmicks and manipulations.

Training Programs

The last approach to motivating employees is to develop a training program based on motivation. At this point, the textbook approach to motivation is often used and the resultant training program is based on those principles and theories. This approach determines that our needs and drives can be identified. It follows that once identified, the manager can appeal to each individual's need or drive, in turn motivating them to excel. The training program deals with five or six needs and possibly ten drives. These needs and drives vary depending on the individual.

The manager is instructed to determine each employee's greatest need or drive. Once this is determined, he then appeals to the needs of the employee through proper job placement and also through daily communication with the employee.

Several problems will develop when this approach is attempted due to the fact that few managers are qualified or have the right to analyze people to this extent. The manager's analysis may also be incorrect. If a manager properly determines the employee's needs, the manager may be unable to appeal to the need. For instance, transferring a person from one job to another because it meets or fulfills his need may be impossible or impractical. An employee may not be qualified to change jobs, the organizational structure may prevent such a move, or the seniority system may be structured such that a move is impossible.

Another problem that will develop when this approach is attempted involves the "drive for security". How can a supervisor-manager appeal to this drive when the employees obtain security from the seniority system, their bargaining efforts, and their contracts? A manager is aware that employees perform just well enough to get by, their security will be ensured.

Consider the "drive for money". With a pay scale there are limits dictated by contract, competition or personnel policies. Under these confines, can the manager pay more for above average or outstanding performance? Substandard performers who occupy identical jobs as outstanding performers will usually, after a period of time, receive the same pay. In this case, the only recourse a manager has is a pat on the back for the outstanding performer and a kick in the rear for the substandard performer. This of course is motivation by recognition of a different kind and will only be effective for a short period of time. Usually, at this point the outstanding performer is promoted into management, thereby losing a good producer and possibly gaining a poor manager.

Determining what drives each employee and how to appeal to his drive can prove to be an interesting and dangerous exercise—with limited success.

The Learning Process

In order to understand the motivational process, it is essential to understand the relationship and the significance of basic learning principles.

This gets back to the development of people. How many training and development programs have we seen where knowledge on a particular subject is passed out to the participants? The instructor or trainer lectures for one or two hours; when finished he relaxes with the feeling that he has passed out "X" amount of knowledge and the participants/students are now knowledgable and educated. Nothing could be farther from the truth.

The learning process consists of three factors or steps. The first step is the acquisition of knowledge. The second step is taking this knowledge and putting it to use in the development of a skill. Once knowledge is developed and skills are learned, change or modification in behavior should follow, completing the third step of the learning process—the development of a good attitude. Again, an attitude is defined as a belief which determines our behavior. Behavior can be modified when beliefs are changed. The learning process is truly accomplished only when each step is completed and there is a good balance between knowledge, skill and attitude. It is fruitless to obtain knowledge and not put it to use to develop a skill. Knowledge without development will not be retained and no positive improvements will result. It is common for managers to possess one or more of these factors and still be unable to gain respect and motivate employees.

Training, Educational and Development Programs must include taking the knowledge and applying it until the skill is developed. Once this is accomplished, knowledge and skill will be retained and confidence will increase to permit the development of a good attitude and proper behavior with an openness to change.

Attitudes

There is another thought in regard to the learning process as it relates to motivation and building of positive attitudes. Quite often the statement is made by supervisors-managers that the attitude of their subordinates is poor. The employees couldn't care less—they don't give a damn. A sobering thought is that the attitude of the employees is a direct reflection of the attitude of their immediate superiors. Management's words and actions create attitudes and employee beliefs. If this thought is accepted, can supervisors and managers blame poor performance and attitudes on their employees?

As stated, proper motivation is dependent of the three steps in the learning process. Unfortunately, a manager is often predestined for failure because of misdirected training programs and the improper attempts at development.

It is a fact that through the years many professionals have said that the three primary contributing causes of accidents are (1) lack of knowledge, (2) inadequate skill, and (3) poor attitude. These are the same contributing causes for poor production and poor quality. In comparing the contributing causes of accidents and poor production with the learning process, it becomes apparent that the entire management process breaks down when there is a weakness in any of these three factors.

An organization's failure to provide each employee with the knowledge and an opportunity to develop the skill will eventually sour a persons attitude. A self-protective device is to then retreat into a familiar group and avoid the unknown and the uncertain. Managers then wonder why some people with strong potential do not want additional responsibility and do not want to take a new job.

An effective manager needs to possess an adequate balance of knowledge, skill and a positive attitude for their particular area of responsibility. Concentration should be on the learning process and on the training and development of each supervisor and manager to obtain the knowledge, develop the skill, and possess the proper attitude to be effective. Once this is accomplished, managers will be able to train employees and become the motivating force.

Respect

In the process of discussing motivation, it is interesting to attempt to determine why some of our well-known political and military national leaders were able to motivate people to respond. Why have certain football coaches been able to demand and obtain excellence in the performance of their players? What does a top manager have that causes good subordinates to say, "I don't always agree with him, but I'd try to go with him if he changed jobs".

In all cases there seems to be one common element—respect for the individual. Why is it that certain people can command and receive respect to the point where subordinates will be motivated to strive to achieve excellence? What determines the difference between a top manager, an average manager, and a poor manager? These questions need to be answered in order to understand motivation. The answer is that the good manager can motivate employees because of his own knowledge, skill, attitude and behavior.

How to Motivate

How does one motivate? How can one attain the position which will qualify him to command respect, obtain cooperation, and initiate the self-drive of the individual to excel? The answer is obvious. A manager can motivate by possessing a sound balance of knowledge, skill, and a positive attitude to conduct themselves in a manner that will command respect and will create in subordinates and superiors the need to actively respond. Once the manager is prepared, he can then understand the importance of each employee's cultural background, the development of the individual, the inherent work factors and proper performance recognition, all of which determine on-the-job behavior.

There are no gimmicks in this thought—only sound management principles. People will respond to the person who has a good balance of knowledge, skill and a positive attitude in the management field. They will respect these individuals because they are qualified.

Limitations

There are limitations in attempting to motivate all people to excel. Possibly the greatest limitation is time. Employees as well as students will respond to sound leadership practices; however, managers and teachers do not have the luxury of time to work with the "five percenters". The five percenters consist of those students and employees that cannot maintain the learning pace of the majority.

The five percenters are those people that are unable or will not respond to the learning process. The size of this group is an estimate and possibly varies from 1-20% depending on their locale. This group enters the educational system often disadvantaged by a culture or a home life lacking in discipline and basic values. They enter the school unable to accept schedules or discipline, have difficulty understanding, and are possibly unable to speak English. Due to the confines of our educational system, the teacher is unable to devote the extra time required to positively motivate and teach the five percenters. As a result of the Civil Rights Act of 1964 as interpreted by the Supreme Court in 1974 in Lau v Nichols, an Hispanic can in some school systems, complete 12 years of school entirely in Spanish.

These five percenters either drop out of the educational system or graduate, unable to read, write, spell, or manage simple arithmetic. The fortunate few obtain a job; however, many do not survive the probationary period. These people cannot comprehend instructions, read orders, or appreciate the necessity to be on time. The five percenters often become a part of the "street environment".

Failure starts in the home. The home environment fails, the educational system fails, and industry is then left with the responsibility to hire and train the five percenters to meet quotas. Does industry have the time and resources to provide training in the three R's? The answer is obvious when qualified applicants are available.

Managers are well aware that not everyone can be motivated to excel. These are the "five percenters" they view as untrainable. Unfortunately, the entire society suffers in the process. Managers are also well aware that individuals possessing basics learning skills and a desire to succeed, will respond to sound leadership principles and practices.

A Basis for Change

Methods used in an attempt to motivate tell alot about the person trying to motivate. Good managers can motivate people because they possess a good balance of knowledge, skill and a positive attitude. These managers have earned the respect and the trust of their employees and are in a position to demand and receive above average performance due to their actions and the type of person they are as individuals.

Low productivity and poor employee attitudes are merely symptoms of the problem. The causes of the problem are the employees' dissatisfaction with their job and their superiors, which has been created by an unsound organizational culture.

A basis for change is present when it is recognized that each level of management directly reflects a person's attitude. It must be accepted that the attitudes of employees about their work situation are formed on the job. As a reflection of the work environment created by management, it is appropriate to ask the tough question: Why are employees motivated not to do what management would prefer? Another axiom that must be accepted is that all employees are motivated. Some, perhaps many, are motivated not to perform as would be preferred. While the organizational culture and work environment elements motivate—positively or negatively—each person responds based on personal beliefs. People are motivated by different elements because of individual needs. As these needs change because of age, the elements that motivate, such as a changing work environment, increased recognition, promotions and high pay, also change.

What motivated a person last year, may no longer be a factor today. Elements that motivate are then a moving target. This requires an individual approach by managers who are trained in the subject and work toward a management technique that recognizes the elements of motivation.

Instead of developing motivational programs based on gimmicks and/or traditional theories, we need to develop managers to be motivators.

Managers need to develop the skills and attitudes to be motivators. Managers need to develop supervisors to be motivators through the acquisition of the necessary knowledge, skills and attitudes to properly control their area of responsibility. Initially, development must be aimed at an individuals immediate responsibilities and then toward future growth.

Motivation is not something special or separate from a manager's total job responsibility. Motivation is a part of the total job and should be treated accordingly. Motivation is not a once a month or periodic shot in the arm. It is a continuous need in any operation. Motivation is a basic part of the management system and is dependent on development programs that concentrate on all the basic management principles as they relate to the job. The best motivating factor is qualified supervisory and management personnel.

1. Donald A. Spartz, "Motivation in Perspective", *Professional Safety*, September 1978, pp. 34-38.
2. A.H. Maslow, *Motivation and Personality*, (New York: Harper & Row, 1954), pp. 80-106.
3. Frederick Herzberg, *The Motivation to Work*, 2nd Edition, (New York: Wiley & Sons, 1959) and *Work and the Nature of Man*, (Cleveland, Ohio: World Publishing Co., 1966).
4. F.J. Roethlisberges and W.J. Dickerson, *Management and the Worker*, (Cambridge, Massachusetts: Harvard University Press, 1939).

10

PRODUCT MARKET WORTHINESS
THE QUALITY CHALLENGE

It is quite obvious that the quality of products made in the United States is of great concern to many companies. One can not clearly define the precise extent to which a number of factors have been responsible for the loss of market share by many U.S. companies. There seems to be wide agreement that the quality of U.S. made products is one of the most significant factors. The loss of market share because of inferior quality would indicate that such products are not worthy to be in the marketplace. The subject of product quality seems to inevitably lead to a discussion of quality control. Because of the complex nature of the quality challenge, a broader discussion of market worthiness will be undertaken.

Any product will succeed if it is deemed, by the user or purchaser, to be worthy of being on the market. Such worthiness means the customer (the often overlooked king) believes the product consistently does what it is supposed to do and delivers a benefit at a cost that is reasonable if not fully competitive. The reliability of the product and its maintainability are implied in the consistent delivery and definition of acceptable product performance.

In trying to cope with the general problems of productivity and quality, U.S. managers frequently find themselves in the frustrating position of attempting to look elsewhere (Japan for example), for their solutions. It is not necessary to dwell on the well-known successes of the Japanese. Nevertheless, the Japanese have not always been looked upon as being successful. What happened over the last several decades that resulted in the productivity and quality successes of the Japanese?

Certainly most management people will recall when a "Made In Japan" label was an indication of a cheap, poorly made product. It was the realization of this image and a decision by the Japanese government and industrial management to make a commitment to change and develop a work environment conducive to participation and respect for quality that paved their way to success.

Many believe that the management techniques successfully used by the Japanese are not transferable to the United States because of cultural differences, although it is generally known that Sony has one of its most efficient production facilities in San Diego, California.

Earlier chapters have provided a framework for new directions in management thinking and application. The subject of product quality is, in the final analysis, a matter of survival for many companies. If a product of inferior quality is produced, and is not worthy of a place in the market, the product and management will fail. An enterprise will be only as successful as its ability to deliver acceptable products to the customer. The challenge for management is significant—it is not overwhelming. The challenge and commitment can be met through some conscious, deliberate management decisions and by providing the leadership to implement the steps needed to create the environment for success.

I believe it is preferable to view the quality challenge within the context of overall management evolution. It has been rather clearly pointed out that a revitalization of management is needed. This need is seen from a very valid perspective. On the other hand, it is timely to suggest that due to changes in the world economy, an expanded and diverse division of the marketplace pie requires an adjustment and reaction. Such changes can be viewed as an evolutionary matter. The need for change by United States management has been recognized for years.

Future change will have to be oriented much more toward the human element as well as toward technology. If the response to this need for change is viewed as a part of the evolution of U.S. management, it may be more acceptable. U.S. firms have found it costly, but otherwise rather simple, to bring about physical and technological change. Change in managing the human element will be less costly, but not as simple. Also, the change now being suggested carries with it the implications that employees have not been well managed. This is another reason change will be difficult to accept and why it will be more palatable if seen in the broader perspective of a natural or evolutionary type process. The implications of the greater consideration of the human element and the support and participation of the entire work force are great in regards to the quality challenge. Some new techniques are suggested but the principles are basic and almost simplistic.

In discussing the quality challenge, it will be helpful to consider several important areas of management involvement:

1. Commitment/Leadership.
2. Design for Quality.
3. Manufacturing/Processing.
4. Quality Control.
5. Quality Assurance.

Commitment/Leadership

It would seem at times that CEO's and senior executives must reach a point of tuning out or feeling overwhelmingly frustrated when they are reminded, on every possible subject, that the ball is always in their court. Nevertheless, the truth of the matter can not be avoided.

It is self-evident that senior management, frequently the CEO alone, sets the tone for the development of their organization's culture.

Quality control failures are usually found to be due to a lack of commitment by top management. It is believed that few CEO's are fully aware of their firm's quality problems or active in setting policy for their solutions.

There are several other axioms to be kept in mind:

• The boss gets what he wants.
• The boss sets the environment in which attitudes are developed.
• The establishment of policy is not synonymous with commitment.
• What actually happens in operations or the work place is usually (almost never) not as effective as those responsible say it is.

The boss is anyone from the CEO down to the first line supervisor. At each level, the axioms apply.

Yes, the boss gets what he wants! He may not always get what he thinks he wants, but he gets what people believe or perceive he wants. Herein lies much of the challenge and need for leadership and direction from the very top. The elements for a sound organizational culture are essential if success in this area is to be achieved.

The impact of what management does and says is significant. Every action, spoken and written word from management, at any level, is given significance—even if it is seemingly unimportant or intended to be insignificant. What people understand or believe to be what the boss wants is what the boss will get. Some examples may help. When line operations supervisors and employees receive directives that constantly stress production—"keep the line moving", "ship products"—the message is clear. The boss wants production even at the expense of quality, safety or equipment failure.

In their book, *In Search of Excellence*, authors Thomas J. Peters and Robert H. Waterman Jr. have rightly outlined the influence of management in their treatment of action, meaning and self-control. They quite clearly state that which has been alluded to or otherwise mentioned:

"Probably few of us would disagree that actions speak louder than words, but we behave as if we don't believe it. We behave as if the proclamation of policy and its execution were synonymous. 'But I made quality our number one goal years ago', goes the lament. Managers can't drive forklifts any more. Yet they still do act. *They do something.* In short, they pay attention to some things and not to others. Their actions express their priorities, and it speaks much louder than words. In the quality case alluded to above, president's subordinate clarified the message, 'of course, he's for quality!' That is, he's never said 'I don't care about quality; it's just that he's for everything.' He says 'I'm for quality,' twice a year and he acts, 'I'm for shipping product twice a day.'"[1]

Actions do indeed speak louder, more eloquently, and more explicitly than words.

In making a commitment to quality (or anything else), the senior executive must recognize and accept the role of leadership in assuring implementation. Policy and procedures are obviously essential. Consistent implementation will happen only when management makes it happen by what it does...does in terms of personally setting the environment and assuring implementation at the line level. Through accountability, delegated responsibility and objective review or audit, the later will be seen as just another application or extension of most in-place management systems. In short, commitment and leadership are not things to be achieved by policy issuances alone, they must be lived in a sound corporate culture that has been developed at the top.

Design for Quality

One of the most significant elements in response to the quality challenge is product design. It is no longer enough to conceive a product and have engineering design ready it for production. Much of the quality and safety problem of products will be resolved on the drawing board. Design considerations should include a number of disciplined reviews by those outside the design function.

Product quality problems, many manifested in product liability claims, require new considerations at the design stage. The results of programmed design reviews through synergistic exercises are promising. The bringing together of marketing, sales, design engineering, manufacturing, purchasing, quality control and legal or insurance representatives for design review at several stages of development, will provide greater assurance for quality and safety. Consideration of the market to be served, sales claims and methods, safety and quality parameters, standards, manufacturing or processing methods, procedures and controls, quality control systems, raw materials or components and potential hazards from use or forseeable misuse are essential. In an open, nonadversarial environment, by drawing upon the collective expertise of the design review participants, much can be accomplished to assure product quality.

As many as 30-40% of all quality control problems may originate in the product's design. Flaws in purchased components are responsible for many product failures. Obviously, these areas need to be analyzed as part of a product quality improvement effort.

Materials from suppliers are as much a source of poor quality as in-house manufacturing problems. It is in the manufacturing area where poor quality components and materials are found.

As one looks back on the so-called decline in the quality of U.S. made products, some interesting facts begin to surface. Was there really a decline in quality? Or, did others set higher quality standards that made the quality of U.S. products appear to be declining? The latter seems to be the case because of built-in obsolesence, and the perceived need to make products as cheaply as possible.

Many of the mea culpas for the sins of "poor quality" are not entirely appropriate. The poor quality did not just happen by fault, it was planned.

Recognizing that designing for obsolesence is passe and no longer acceptable, management which made previous design decisions must now reverse those decisions.

Manufacturing/Processing

It was mentioned that causes of poor quality are many times traced to the production floor. While that is true, the cause for poor quality, as was also mentioned, is not directly attributable to those in control of the manufacturing processes.

The responsibility of manufacturing is to produce the product per the design specifications, using the materials, components, equipment and procedures typically provided by others.

Manufacturing and processing controls and procedures are essential and play a significant role in product quality. There must be an environment that respects people and their comfort and one that is generally clean and adequately equipped and maintained. Nonconforming materials and parts should be identified and segregated from the production area. The substitution of materials or components, a source of product failure, must be effectively controlled. Frequently, line employees and supervisors make substitutions that result in inferior or even unsafe products. All substitutions or changes in manufacturing procedures must be controlled by and coordinated with design engineering.

In too many manufacturing operations, managers are caught in a trap or otherwise find themselves in an adversarial relationship with quality control, production control, marketing, sales and engineering. Many of the problems in the manufacturing process can be avoided in the early design reviews. The results of synergistic efforts during design and other areas of operations are potentially the most significant contributions to the solution of the quality and productivity problems. Again, the environment for this to happen will have to be created and maintained by management.

Employees and even supervisors are overlooked in the process of seeking solutions to problems—usually because of the overall environment that discourages participation.

Workers can think and they can make contributions. After all, who knows best how to build a product or component at the production level? The input or participation of employees is a resource too infrequently tapped by management. In solving the quality and productivity problem, it is not always a matter of acquiring additional resources. The most important resource is already in place—people who will participate in an encouraging environment.

The dissatisfaction with authoritarian management and the message received from management—keep the line going, ship product—provides great challenges. These elements must be changed if market worthiness is to be achieved.

Workers are frequently heard to complain about the lack of quality parts and components. They are critical of maintenance procedures. Mostly, they are critical of the steps taken by management to correct quality problems. It is not unusual to find a corporate or outside consultant brought in to suggest solutions. These "solutions" are forced downward, reluctantly accepted by managers and supervisors and often sabotaged by the workers.

The Japanese are more likely to move from the bottom up. They involve those closest to the problem and discourage confrontation. As each level or department agrees on what should be done, conclusions are pushed upward through the ranks.

There are indications that many managers see automation, robotics and computerization as solutions to the quality and productivity challenge at the manufacturing level. The contrary could well be the case if total reliance is placed on new technology. The application of new technology will require an even greater attention to the human element. More educated, sophisticated and highly-skilled people will expect or even demand an open entrepreneurial-participative environment in which they will choose to spend their work day. They will make themselves heard and management will be wise to assure surroundings of down/up and lateral communication and participative direction of the work place.

Management will also need to recognize and adjust to the long and short-term goals within the organization. At the top, goals are generally long-term, especially in relation to the short-term goals at the production or manufacturing level. Written or not, day-to-day goals in production are short-term. Each day the primary goal is to produce a certain number of units.

In being sensitive to the short-term goals of operating employees, management can not assume that their long-term goals are understood or accepted by people, even in the middle management structure. The need here is to establish a management style that is attentive and responsive to the daily goals and routines at the manufacturing level.

One response from management that has surfaced is understandable. That is the feeling of relinquishing prerogatives and abdicating responsibility. Largely, these fears are unfounded and need not be of great concern if honest, deliberate efforts to foster participation are made.

In their research of successful companies, *In Search of Excellence* authors Peters and Waterman came to the conclusion that successful firms do not mollycoddle the employee. Rather, they found:

"We are talking about tough-minded respect for the individual and the willingness to train him, to set reasonable and clear expectations for him, and to grant him practical autonomy to step out and contribute directly to his job. Genuine people orientation is in marked contrast to the two major alternatives all too often seen in companies; the lip service disaster and the gimmick diaster."[2]

An introspective analysis by managers at all levels with deliberate consideration of the "do as I say - not as I do" or other authoritarian conduct, will require little more to be said about lip service. In regard to the gimmick trap, the authors went on to say:

"The current gimmick is the quality circle. There is absolutely nothing wrong with the idea, as the Japanese have so forcefully reminded us. But quality circles are only the latest in a long line of tools

99

that can either by very helpful, or can simply serve as a smoke screen while management continues to get away with not doing its job of real people involvement."[3]

Perhaps there has been an overemphasis on the development of rules, procedures and demands that have an underlying theme: Employees are lazy, they cheat, they don't want to give a day's work for a day's pay, etc., etc. This management response results in an environment that demoralizes the majority of the work force when a small percentage of people may actually, but rarely, fit the above description, given the right climate in which to work.

In designing for change and revitalizing the manufacturing environment, a good starting point could be the analysis of rules and procedures, questioning why they were developed in the first place. With a genuine move toward respect for people, many, if not most, of the rules and procedures could be dropped.

Quality Control

It has been clearly established that any improvement in quality goes well beyond the scope and activity of the quality control function. Nevertheless, this function will be a critical element in any effort to improve quality and the market worthiness of a product.

If upper management is as confused about the role of quality control as those in quality control and manufacturing, there is little wonder why this function seems to suffer in many organizations.

What is the role of quality control? It is always interesting to listen and read on this subject. Some will state emphatically that the role of quality control is to assure delivery of a safe, high quality product to the customers.

Others will state, just as emphatically, that quality control's role is to assure the building or production of the product in line with the design and manufacturing specifications. Still others believe the role is to merely inspect and test per the quality control manual. The latter is probably more prevalent than we realize.

Though there are exceptions, the typical role of quality control is to assure, insofar as practical, that the product is made to design specifications, that specified manufacturing procedures are followed, designated materials are used, and that the product will pass certain performance or design tests.

What this means is most significant and frequently not understood. In other words, if a product design is weak, quality control will assure the delivery of a weak product. If there is a defect in design, quality control will assure that the defect will be built into the product. If there is a safety related defect in design, quality control will assure the finished product to be unsafe. Certainly, management will righteously respond by saying, that's not what we intended, although that is the end result in many organizations.

The whole aspect of quality control provides a fascinating subject for discussion. Manufacturing management is typically at odds with quality control and vice versa. Quality control people press for more inspectors and testing equipment. Manufacturing people claim there are already too many inspections and inspectors. Who is right?

The publication *First-Line Management* states one objective of quality control is "...to assure that the customer will receive the quality product promised him by the sales and engineering departments. Since quality is built into a product or service, it is necessary to begin the quality control system at the very beginning—during the product engineering phase".[4]

This text for manufacturing engineers goes on to say:

"On the surface it would appear that the foreman has little to do with delivering a well-designed product. On the contrary, however, he plays a most important part. In most companies the foreman is looked to for information which, when fed back to the engineering department, can assist in the alleviation of engineering problems."[5]

These points support the premise that design, rather than quality control, provides the most promise for product quality improvement.

These same points also provide the basis for another observation about the production versus quality control clashes. The same text expands that aspect:

"The mere mention of quality control in the company of foremen often evolves a strong reaction. Despite the protestations of both sides, it sometimes appears that both the inspection department and the foremen enjoy the "contests" with which they become involved. These "contests" may be constructive, though in most cases they are not, and almost inevitably they result in negative behavior which does not enhance or assist in maintaining quality."[5]

Quality can not be inspected into a product. This old axiom is as appropriate today as it was many years ago when it was first heard.

Did you ever wonder why some companies advertise the fact that they have legions of quality control inspectors? And that their products are inspected zillions of times during and after manufacture? This may sound impressive to some, but many knowledgeable people may question their claims and their products. For example, why do such enormous resources need to be devoted to detecting quality problems? What is there in the product's design and manufacture that requires so many inspections and tests? Could not production employees find the problems? Such advertising is paradoxical and filled with inconsistency. Management would be well advised to raise some questions and take some action if there are indicators of these kinds within the organization. Some would suggest that the number of quality control inspections or inspectors is reflective of the basic quality built into the design and manufacturing steps. The more inspectors, the greater the quality problem in many cases.

An overabundance of inspections implies a lack of confidence in manufacturing management and production management. By reinforcing what may already be an adversarial relationship between manufacturing and quality control, people will play games that go beyond a "contest".

Reliance on inspections for quality will be a crutch for employees and managers. It will provide an excuse or be used as a cop-out by others. The authority and responsibility of workers and managers is frequently usurped by over inspection. Remember, quality can not be inspected into the product. Quality must be designed in by design engineering and built in by the work force. Too much reliance on the quality control function is unwise, unnecessary and damaging to the kind of environment required to correct the quality problem.

The findings of a poll published in *Manufacturing Productivity Frontiers* provides additional data for consideration. For example:

"The polling of business experts showed that Japanese manufacturers have the best reputation for quality. The United States was rated tenth behind a cluster of European countries and New Zealand. Britain was viewed as next to the worst country after Greece in this regard. Also included under dynamics of the market was advertising expenditure. The United States spent more than any other country on per capita advertising, but Japan ranked only thirteenth."[6]

Could it be that advertising expenditures might be better utilized and perhaps channeled into other areas for development, design and quality. The dynamics of the market place will determine the customer's perceptions of quality; not advertising.

The role played by quality control in relation to the product liability problem bears expansion.

Quality control and product safety or liability prevention are not synonymous. The number of product liability claims and the amount of awards are heavy burdens for many U.S. manufacturers. Invariably, in discussing this subject, reference is made to quality control as if it were the primary requirement for product safety. As has been suggested earlier, it could be one of the deterrents and a false security blanket.

In numerous costly product liability cases, defective design, rather than manufacturing defect, was the basis for an award to the injured plaintiff. If the quality control function is merely charged to assure manufacture in accordance with design, the full potential of the function is not being realized. In a broader context of quality assurance, this potential could be realized profitably. This will be expanded later.

Another point on quality control. The fact that manufacturing management and quality control are frequently at odds is rather well established. The organizational structure within which these entities report deserves some review. If, for example, the Quality Control Department reports to manufacturing management, look out. While it is possible for such an arrangement to work, it is highly probable that weaknesses exist and quality suffers under that arrangement. Such a situation is akin to allowing the Payroll Department to determine their own pay increases.

A quality control function should report to a level similar to internal audit, usually to a top level of management. If management is serious about quality, it will have to allow the control function a wide latitude in having direct contact with all operating departments. When it speaks, it should speak with the authority and influence of upper management.

Finally, did you ever consider a quality control function that monitors the quality of the Quality Control Department? As in other areas of operations, quality control is susceptible to mismanagement and weaknesses.

It is not necessary to establish another management system, but an objective review and audit of the quality control function is warranted. In making audits of product liability prevention, the analysis of the quality control functions is included. It is not unusual to find well developed, complete quality control manuals. It is likewise not unusual to find that they are not always followed. Phantom inspections have been uncovered. Procedures for inspection and testing have been by-passed or changed without approval from design or top management. The records required for documentation have not always been completed. In other words, the shortcomings which some people seem to develop may be present in all functions, including quality control. Objective audits by detached or disinterested professionals are highly recommended.

Quality Assurance

There would seem to be general agreement that a quality control function is essential to the successful delivery of a satisfactory or superior product. We have also established that the Quality Control Department may have been wrongly perceived to be the main key to quality production. The role of quality control is, in fact, rather narrow in most cases. The friction between quality control and manufacturing is an inhibitor to quality, most seem to agree. What then, can be done organizationally to set up the mechanics to get all entities pulling together and in the same direction? Quality assurance, which is more than a concept, may be the solution to be considered by many managements.

There are many firms with quality assurance units or departments. The activity varies greatly from company to company and with the nature of the products. But they all have a common goal, to assure the quality of the product, not merely to inspect it.

The broad nature of quality assurance provides the flexibility for quality decisions and planning that goes far beyond the typical quality control function. Such flexibility on a broad scale was found many years ago to be needed in the manufacture of military goods, aircraft and aerospace products. The nuclear industry is heavily reliant on a broad quality assurance system. Obviously, the nature of the operations mentioned above will not provide a practical framework for general industry. Don't be turned off by this. It is not necessary to add another layer of bureaucracy, and visions of large staff increases are unwarranted. There are some proven concepts in the quality assurance idea that hold promise for quality improvement for even the smallest organizations, without the need for expanded staff. In fact, effective quality assurance activity may well make it possible to allocate some manpower elsewhere.

By necessity, quality assurance units are highly structured in some firms due to the size of operations and the critical nature of the product. It is not our intent to address such kinds of operations, but rather, to expand on a variety of activities that will apply to most manufacturing situations.

The real value of an effective quality assurance function is not confined to the end results, that being a quality product. The very nature of the activity undertaken, on a scale that touches every level of an organization, results in the building of an effective team that can be brought to bear on virtually any problem related to productivity and quality.

In his writings, George Strauss of the University of California says of the manufacturing manager's position:

"The manufacturing manager's authority will decline. Indeed, he may become just another member of the team, and perhaps not the most

104

important one. Manufacturing and product engineering will have to work more closely; perhaps the difference between the two will decline."[7]

Thomas R. Horton, as President of the American Management Association, made these observations about corporate organization to Edwin Darby, Financial Columnist at the *Chicago Sun Times*:

"I do think that in the United States we developed a bureaucratic mentality. We call it the layered corporation or the laminated corporation, one layer of management on top of another. One estimate is that management in a United States Corporation may number three times as many people as a similar company in Germany or Japan.

"Where the Japanese have overtaken us is not in research of innovation 'or even in the much-touted Japanese approach to management' but in manufacturing technique, quality control and cost control."[8]

A well managed quality assurance function treats each of these areas which are cited as significant reasons for the Japanese success. In dealing with internal entities that have traditionally been separately managed, new approaches and changes in management systems, and in particular, management styles will be necessary.

Some layers of the management structure will need to be treated in a system of overlap or blending so the distinctions become less pronounced or disappear entirely.

The term "synergistics" is much used and just as much misunderstood. In the manufacturing environment, synergism could be another term for cooperation that is a bit formalized or structured and interactive. In any case, it will always hold true that the sum of the whole of a cooperative group is greater than the sum of the individual parts of the group. This is true synergism, getting greater results from a group than can be separately obtained from each individual. Participative management has the same potential but rarely has it been tapped.

In earlier discussions on design review, the value of synergistic groups was mentioned. One of the main functions of quality assurance is to pull together the right people from various disciplines for quality and safety design reviews. Different team members will participate at different stages of a review. As new products are conceived and before pencil is used on the drawing board, a conceptual design review is in order. The quality assurance leader will bring together the marketing, sales, manufacturing, design, purchasing, quality control, insurance, safety or legal representatives to review the idea and to identify points to be addressed if the idea is pursued.

In future reviews when designs are put on paper and when prototypes are developed, other disciplines or operating departments will be part of the quality assurance team.

Quality assurance, under the leadership of an executive thoroughly knowledgeable about the firm, its goals and capabilities, will be able to address product quality, production efficiency and product safety, using the collective brains of each appropriate unit.

In addition to setting the stage for and conducting design reviews, the quality assurance function will provide direction for some deliberate consideration of a multitude of concerns. These might include market feasibility, sales approaches, advertising needs and constraints, raw materials and component availability, evaluation of suppliers, developing quality control manuals, systems and tests, manufacturing equipment needs, manufacturing methods, employee training needs, packaging and shipping concerns. Virtually everyone of these areas, each usually managed as a separate entity, affect product quality, product safety and product liability.

Through a quality assurance approach, where functions are given wide latitude in a synergistic environment, a multitude of quality issues can be effectively managed.

Quality Control Circles

Only limited reference will be made in this chapter to quality control circles (QCC's). Other chapters have given them some mention. A brief treatment here is warranted.

Quality control circles are not new. Many U.S. firms have used them for some years. Quality control circles were imported by the Japanese where the success level is not as high as some might suggest. In the United States, there have been many more quality circle failures than successes.

Matthew Goodfellow of the University Research Center, Chicago, writes in *Manufacturing Engineering*:

"After studying twenty-nine American companies with QCC programs, we found that most were unsuccessful. Only eight of the twenty-nine produced satisfactory results."[9]

Woodruff Imberman writes in *Canadian Business*:

"Our own (Imberman and Deforest) two year forty-one company study involved manufacturers, distributors, retailers and insurance companies. We found that only thirteen of the programs met the test of positive financial payback."[10]

106

The failures resulted because QCC's were viewed as a single answer to the quality challenge, usually in a stifling, rather than an open, environment. Without a genuine organization wide, top to bottom organizational culture that promotes involvement and participation, quality control circles are doomed to failure. It is not the mere existence of quality control circles that brings the sought after results. Rather, it is the culture, tone, environment, openness to participation and all the similar things that are needed to allow quality control circle ideas to bear fruit.

In all probability, quality control circles will follow the pattern of the demise of other potentially valuable management tools such as management by objectives. Why? Because the idea of participative decision making can not be accepted by the traditional manager.

On the other hand, if an open, participative environment exists and the organizational culture is employee, customer and product oriented, the value of organized quality control circles would be unlimited. In such an environment, the benefits of quality control circles would probably be already realized.

One of the great benefits of an effective quality assurance system is its ability to accomplish many of the objectives of quality control circles. The effective quality assurance approach includes sincere solicitation and concerted effort to obtain employee input about operating problems, quality, and other related matters. Front line supervisors, often overlooked, are also brought prominently into the picture by quality assurance. The most important element, the customer, provides much direction to the activities of a quality assurance function. Customer cases of satisfaction and dissatisfaction are aggressively sought. Customer complaints receive great attention in a well directed quality assurance system.

The Supplier

In one sense, every enterprise is a supplier. At the same time, every enterprise is a customer. Remember, the customer is king! This means that you as a manufacturer can and should demand to be a satisfied customer. Yet, there are ample indications that many times, quality suffers because of the less than satisfactory performance of suppliers of raw materials and components.

When faulty materials from suppliers are accepted, the internal efforts to achieve or improve quality are negated. When managers accept faulty material from suppliers, the message relayed to supervisors and production employees is clear. The message is that management isn't really serious about the quality challenge.

The successful quality assurance function will not only be content to sample or test certain incoming supplies. The quality control efforts of the supplier will be evaluated at the supplier's production line. An analysis and audit of the effectiveness of the supplier's quality control will be undertaken.

Several suppliers of comparable or similar materials will be reviewed and graded for the potential to deliver high quality raw materials or components. Quality assurance will establish identification specifications for raw materials and supplies so that nonconforming goods can be readily traced to their source.

There is, except perhaps in a few cases, little need for management to be overly concerned with devoting significant additional financial, physical or human resources to improve the market worthiness or quality of products. The greatest need is for change in the directions suggested throughout these pages. Once such change is sincerely accomplished, the productivity, efficiency, and quality challenges will have been met.

1. Thomas J. Peters and Robert H. Waterman Jr., *In Search of Excellence*, (New York: Harper & Row, 1982) p. 73.
2. Ibid., p. 239.
3. *In Search of Excellence,* p. 241.
4. Dr. Donald R. Kirkpatrick, *First Line Management*, (Dearborn, Michigan: Society of Manufacturing Engineers, 1972) p. 44.
5. Ibid., p. 45.
6. Dr. Hikaru Kerns, "Japan Wins - By A Mile", *Manufacturing Productivity Frontier*, Volume 6, No. 3 (Chicago: Illinois Institute of Technology, March 1982) p. 31.
7. George Strauss, "Manufacturing Organizations for the Future", *Organization for Manufacturing*, (Dearborn, Michigan: Society of Manufacturing Engineering, 1970) p. 232.
8. Edwin Darby, "Bureacuracy Hides Marketplace Reality", *Chicago Sun Times,* July 7, 1982, p. 64.
9. Dr. Matthew Goodfellow, "Quality Control Circle Programs - What Works and What Doesn't", *Manufacturing Engineering*, September 1981, (Dearborn, Michigan: Society of Manufacturing Engineers) pp. 70-72.
10. Woodruff Imberman, "Why Quality Control Circles Don't Work", *Canadian Business*, Volume 55, No. 5, (Toronto, Canada: CB Media Limited, May 1982), pp. 103-106.

11

A QUALITY STORY

The preceding chapter laid the ground work and guidelines for an organization to revitalize and develop to achieve measurable results in improving productivity. What results can an organization expect by initiating a Development Program tailored to specific needs with elements designed to achieve specific agreed upon goals? The answer depends on an organization's present status.

Quality Steel in Bensenville, Illinois, provides a case study of the results from a development process based on sound, proven, basic principles of management.[1] In 1976 the importance of developing people was identified as the key to reducing worker compensation costs and improving productivity from the bottom up. Development was recognized as absolutely essential if, as a privately owned corporation, Quality Steel was to grow, expand and maintain an edge over competition.

The entire program was based on four productivity improvement factors: (1) the manager, based on his supervisory skills or lack of them, is the greatest motivating factor or the greatest hinderance, (2) the organizational culture, defined as the attitudes and practices of management, including open candid communications; objectivity in relating to others; listening skills; ability to critique; and the ability to obtain employee participation and agreed on Standards of Performance to determine results, (3) the importance of addressing the contributing causes of productivity problems vs. dealing with the symptoms, (4) a program based on sound basic management principles, avoiding gimmicks such as the theory on proper lifting techniques, promotional material or awards, or programs like the recent quality circle fad.

Organizations dealing solely with unsafe procedures are dealing with the symptoms of the problem and not the cause, and as a result, are fighting fires. Our approach was to deal with the "reasons why" there are production problems, unsafe procedures and conditions. This meant dealing with the contributing causes of (a) lack of knowledge, (b) inadequate skills, and (c) poor attitude, with attitude being defined as a "belief" which determines behavior. A supervisor-manager cannot be expected to perform if he does not have the necessary knowledge and supervisory-managerial skills to identify and change negative attitudes and beliefs toward a more positive position. The importance of addressing the causes of productivity problems vs. dealing with the symptoms is shown by the Loss Sequence illustrated in *Figure 11-1*.

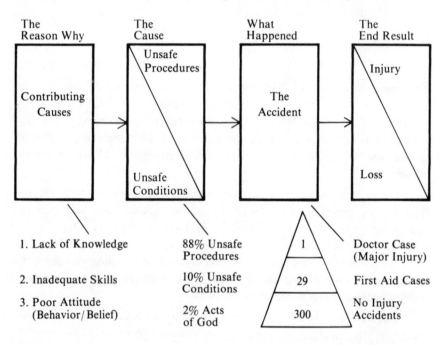

Figure 11-1. The Loss Sequence

The Development Program

The decision to initiate a Supervisory-Management Development Program was made by Howard Berman, President, and Robert Gifford, Vice President of Operations for Quality Steel Processing.

The program consisted of a 12 month comprehensive Supervisory-Management Development Program. The program objectives were:

1. The development of positive attitudes and expectations in order to instill pride in themselves as members of management and to provide a positive impact on productivity.

2. Improve each participants communications skills with emphasis on listening, questioning, nonverbal communication and obtaining employee feedback.
3. Improving the management skills of the supervisory staff, including skill in handling employees, resolving conflicts, decision making, enforcing work rules on a uniform basis and improving employee and management relations.
4. Preparing the supervisory staff to train employees through proper job instruction. Priority was placed on administrative operational procedures, which account for a high percentage of production errors.
5. The development of a Job Analysis Program to identify, eliminate and/or control unsafe and nonproductive job procedures. This would then be used as a part of the program to train employees.
6. The individual development of clearly defined Standards of Performance. This would identify responsibilities and the performance standards for each supervisor. This resulted in an objective method of measuring individual performance and identifying specific training and development needs.
7. Train supervisors to effectively control accidents and reduce the Workers' Compensation medical-disability cost to less than $700 per each 10,000 manhours worked.

These objectives were to be achieved by conducting in-plant group sessions with supervisors and key managers. In addition, one-on-one, on-the-job assistance was provided to monitor and to ensure that change in behavior actually took place.

Elements of the Program

Elements of the Supervisory-Manager Skill Development Program as outlined below were sequenced to achieve immediate results in reducing accidents and gradually improving productivity.

PHASE I

Attitudes and the Development Process
Attitude Status Determination.
Attitude Development and Modification Factors.
Productivity Trends.
The Learning Process.
Coaching.
Proper Job Instruction.

111

Expectations and Productivity.
Developing and Obtaining a Commitment.
Professionalism.

PHASE II

Motivation

Traditional Approaches—Theory vs. Need.
Maslow's Hierarchy of Human Needs.
Human Factors—Application in the Real World.
Practical Application—Proven Approaches.

Communication

The Communication Process.
Principles and Practices.
The Essential Elements of Communication.
Questioning.
Listening.
Interviewing Techniques.

PHASE III

Group Performance

Communication...continued

Nonverbal Communication.
Employee Feedback.
Performance Evaluation.
Problem Identification and Problem Solving.
The Decision Making Process.
Delegation and Developing a Climate of Trust.

PHASE IV

Leadership and Management

The Nature of Management.
Leadership and Respect.
The Management System.
Leadership Styles.
Safety Responsibility.
Investigation.
Job Analysis and Control Procedures.
Leadership in Conducting Meetings.
Work Rule Enforcement.
Discipline.

PHASE V

Self-Management

Time Management.
Responsibility vs. Authority.
Instruction Techniques.
Self-Assessment.
Operating Budgets.
Determining Career Development Needs.
Self-Development.
The Power of Goals.
Measuring Results.
The Impact of the Supervisor.

As the development of the program proceeded, the emphasis shifted from safety to quality, services, schedules, rejects, equipment maintenance, breakdowns, and communication barriers. The same process as illustrated in the Loss Sequence in *Figure 11-1* was used with these problems. The "Accident" data can be erased and any problem area inserted to allow managers to identify the reasons why productivity problems occur. Once this thought process is developed, action can be taken to prevent recurring problems and provide long-term effects.

In the years prior to starting the program, one costly area was "back injuries". We firmly believe, and our studies and analysis over the years confirm our belief, that the majority of the reported injuries increased after emphasis was placed on the so-called proper lifting techniques. Working with organizations experiencing an upward trend in back claims, we discovered that after an organization had completed a campaign on "safe and proper lifting techniques", there was a sudden increase in back injuries.

Medical experts long ago determined that the human back starts to deteriorate in our mid 30s. With the emphasis organizations placed on safe lifting techniques and with the pain and injury which results from improper lifting, employees experiencing discomfort naturally felt they had sustained back injuries caused from on-the-job lifting.

It is my opinion, with which not everyone agrees, that lifting in the long recommended manner of keeping one's back straight and using one's legs to lift has placed workers in an unnatural position. I believe this has caused many back injuries which has resulted in unnecessary Workers' Compensation claims and high dollar losses.

Our approach in training supervisors to instruct their employees as to proper lifting techniques, was to maintain a low profile. As a result, our entire safe lifting program can be stated in one sentence: "Lift in whatever position is comfortable to you but never beyond your capability". Emphasis was placed on engineering and providing proper material handling equipment. This approach has worked with many organizations and proved to be effective at Quality Steel. Since 1976, back injuries have been almost nil with only complaints of minor strains, and with no lost work time.

In Phase IV, Leadership and Management, emphasis was placed on Job Analysis and Job Control Procedures. We have found that the research published by W.H. Heinrich in 1931[2] is valid. Mr. Henrich found that 88% of the accidents were caused by unsafe acts, which we refer to as unsafe procedures.

Job Analysis

Numerous major companies with excellent safety programs and corresponding results have been using a Job Analysis (JA) for many years. Briefly, the JA Program involves (1) determining and listing the steps and procedures the employee uses in his job, (2) identifying the hazards and/or production problems in each step of his job, (ideally the hazard or the problem will be eliminated at this point), where elimination is not possible or practical then, (3) a Job Control Procedure is established so the employee can work without being injured or causing production problems.

The benefits of the JA Program are as follows:
1. Establishes the proper job procedures to be followed. If procedures account for 88% of all accidents, quality and production problems, then proper job procedures becomes an important factor.
2. Identifies the hazards and/or production problems in each procedural step of the job.
3. Permits elimination of job hazards and production problems.
4. Where job hazards or production problems cannot be eliminated, then a Job Control Procedure can be established. It is only fair to an employee to make him aware of the hazards and problems involved in his job, so he will know how to work without being injured or causing production and quality problems.
5. Provides a formal training guide for new and old employees. If training is to be accomplished, we should concentrate on what is most important to the employee's safety and productivity of his total job.
6. Provides supervision with an easy visual check of the procedures the employee is following.
7. Permits employee participation and communication involving job

114

procedures. Prior to each JA being finalized, the employee on the job must review the steps, hazards, and control measures to ensure that they are correct. The employee knows his job better than anyone, therefore, his input and approval is important.

8. Assists in establishing the cause in accident investigations. When an accident does occur, it is easy to use the JA to determine the actual cause, whether the accident was due to an unsafe procedure, an unsafe condition or both.

9. Assist an employee in planning his job.

10. When a new supervisor is assigned to a department, he has the JA available for ready reference material to assist in his new responsibilities.

Success stories with companies using the Job Analysis Program are numerous. In almost every Job Analysis conducted, previously unknown quality and production problems were identified and either eliminated or controlled.

Job Control

Acceptance of the Job Analysis Program was increased by obtaining employee participation and by dealing with the total job. Once the Job Analysis was completed, it then became a Job Control Procedure. If we believe that safety and production go hand-in-hand, then all steps in the job need to be included in the Job Analysis. Is the program worth it? Will it slow down production? Results tell the story.

In May of 1977, Quality Steel completed the Job Analysis Program as part of the Supervisory-Management Development and Control Program. The company had been averaging 5.25 disabling injuries each year. Over a 12 month period, results of the program showed a 43% increase in production, manhours per ton of steel processed was reduced by 22%, and the entire plant worked without a single disabling injury. The Job Analysis Program was a contributing factor in achieving these measurable results.

Once the basic program was completed, our service evolved to one of assisting, advising and monitoring vs. conducting and managing the program.

Figure 11-2 illustrates the annual lost time accident incident rates. The OSHA national average is presently 4.9.

The reduction in accidents as illustrated in *Figure 11-2,* means a reduction in dollar losses as illustrated in *Figure 11-3*. As a result of being able to control their losses, the company was able to insure their workers compensation liability with a three year retrospective plan. This resulted in

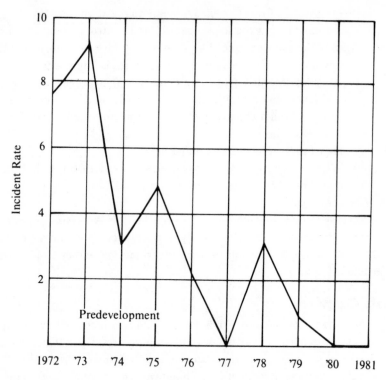

Figure 11-2. Annual Lost Time Accident Incident Rate

sizable dollar returns on their premiums paid for each of the three years. Their present worker compensation premium now runs about 65% less. These are dollars which are added directly to the bottom line. This is particularly impressive in light of inflation and the increased benefit levels for injured workers.

The most objective method of measuring safety performance is with the Experience Modification Factor (EMF).[3] This factor measures, by industry, an organization's accident dollar losses over a three year period. In each industry, the average is 1.00 with anything higher being rated as worse than the average. Quality Steel's EMF was 1.50 before the program was implemented. Their EMF is now 0.69 which means they are better than average for their industry. In fact, it means they came from being 50% worse than average to being 31% better than average.

Figure 11-4 illustrates Quality Steel's results in shop manhours per ton of steel processed.

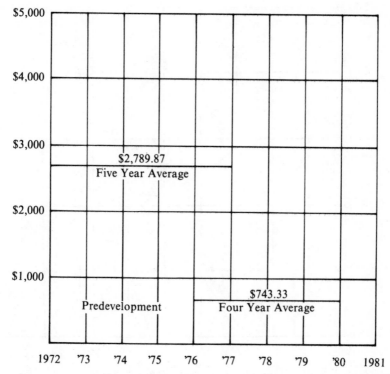

Figure 11-3. Worker's Compensation Medical-Disability Cost Per Each 10,000 Manhours Worked

Quality Steel has experienced a growth trend through the development of sound, basic management principles. The emphasis on developing supervision and employees has opened up communications and improved the working environment. Employee participation is sought, is encouraged and has improved with an increased sense of pride in the quality and service they provide to their customers.

Clients have a right to privacy, however, we can say that since 1976, Quality Steel's sales have more than tripled. Their profit picture follows an upward trend.

A great deal more than a Supervisor-Manager Development Program is involved in Quality Steel's success story. However, this program is a part of and is basic to the success in starting the process of developing a sound organizational culture which permits growth and increases profits.

We thank Quality Steel for permission to print their story. Management's

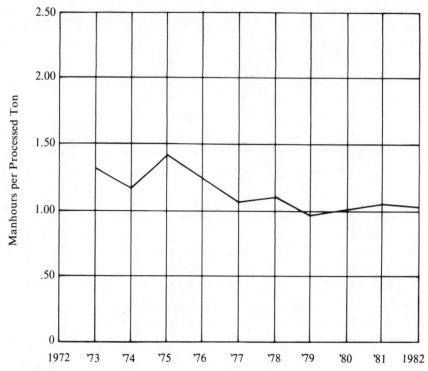

Figure 11-4. Shop Manhours per Ton of Steel Processed

commitment with visible involvement in bringing about a change on a sound, systematic basis has been successful. Quality Steel has now started a new developmental phase toward Participative Team Management.

Robert Gifford, Vice President of Operations at Quality Steel provides a conclusion to this "Quality Story":

"From its inception in 1963, Quality Steel has operated under a basic philosophy of performing all of our tasks with a goal of being the best in every area in which we must participate to be a quality company. Our very name implies this and we strive for this.

"We have as an operating theorem here, to break down each job or task into its most basic unit, analyze it, revise it, and implement change. Sort of a 'work smarter, not harder' and 'who knows more about how a job should be done than the very man doing it' approach. Over the years we have followed this basic philosophy and have enjoyed the benefits of our labor. We have been very successful in developing a viable organization at all levels, from the very top to our basic, entry level positions in the shop. Perhaps the catalyst in this philosophy is the participative team approach to solve quality and production problems. Under this philosophy, we challenge all the old, time-honored methods of running a business to create a much more effective management style which allows change to occur without the usual roadblocks found in most organizations.

"Our top executives, including the Chairman, make it a practice to spend time on the floor listening to and observing employees. The employees responded by feeling a part of the organization and became commited to quality and service. This has improved our communications, and caused our morale and motivation to excel.

"We have found that change from within, using the participative team approach can, in some instances, be much more effective if an external stimulus is used. This can be in the form of a manager who has successfully implemented this approach from another division outside the plant in question. Another approach would be to employ an outside consultant who is thoroughly familiar with the participative team approach. Since we are all fighting the battle of improved quality and productivity, it is imperative that a course of action is established and the battle begun."

1. Donald A. Spartz, "Training Managers to Monitor Safety", *Metal Center News,* January 1983, p. 28.
2. W.H. Heinrich, *Industrial Accident Prevention,* (McGraw Hill Book Co., 1931).
3. D.A. Weaver, *An Updated Index to Safety Performance* (Park Ridge, Illinois: Professional Safety, December 1972), pp. 23-28.

12

PARTICIPATIVE TEAM MANAGEMENT SKILLS

In the chapter entitled, "*Creating an Environment for Change*", Participative Team Management (PTM) is mentioned as a part of the Strategic Organization Revitalization Plan. Through team building, Participative Team Management is one of the major elements in developing more effective managers and improving productivity. Participative Team Management permits and fosters the best solutions and management practices toward developing and maintaining a sound organizational culture. The results involve barriers being removed, problems are identified and solved, conflicts are confronted and resolved, with creativity and change becoming a way of managing.

Defining and communicating what constitutes Participative Team Management is difficult. Mention the term to a group of supervisors-managers and most will indicate that they are team managers, they practice team management concepts, cooperate, work together and get along well. "In reality, people confuse team management with conformity. A decision is made, a policy is set, and be it right or wrong, everyone falls in line and conforms. There is no room for discussion, conflicts are suppressed, creativity is discouraged. Sound team management concepts and practices are much more complex".[1]

Traffic lights in Waterloo, Iowa are used to illustrate what can happen when Participative Team Management is not in effect. Twenty years ago, traveling through Waterloo on Route 218 was an experience. The traffic lights were not synchronized and each light operated independently. Driving through the town in heavily jammed traffic was a stop and go process, with cross traffic very light or nonexistent. Tempers would flare, fenderbender's were frequent, time was lost and energy consumed. Even in the early hours of the day, it seemed impossible to make it through two consecutive lights without stopping. As a result, travelers would drive extra miles to bypass and avoid traveling through Waterloo, Iowa.

Certainly the city engineers felt they were doing a good job as all the traffic lights were engineered, installed, and working as planned. They had fulfilled one of their many job responsibilities. The engineers, administration officials, and politicians were independently doing their jobs well.

Some years later, while using this story as an example in a meeting, a resident of Waterloo interrupted and informed the group that the lights were now synchronized. In spite of this, old attitudes and impressions remain, and to this day travelers will drive the extra miles to avoid Waterloo, Iowa.

Imagine Waterloo as a manufacturing concern. Each traffic light is a first line supervisor-manager responsible for controlling the flow of material, quality, safety, and proper utilization of capital, natural, and human resources. A supervisor-manager could report that material is piling up, it's coming too fast, there is too much work and he can't process it all. A second supervisor-manager can be advised that his department is not busy and he had better find out what is wrong. Each supervisor-manager starts blaming the preceeding supervisor-manager, the shipping and receiving supervisors-managers, and staff personnel. Conflicts and problems continue to create adversarial working relationships. The workers develop attitudes that reflect the process.

Management by Conformance

Each supervisor-manager communicates to their superiors by asking for help and each is told to solve their own problems, to make efficient use of the equipment that has been engineered and installed as required, and to learn how to get along and manage more effectively. With this type of feedback and nonassistance from their superiors, there will be fewer complaints. At this point, communication becomes downward and restricted. The supervisors, engineers, support personnel and middle-managers will all learn to conform. They believe they are now team players as they cooperate, work together and get along well. Never mind that in some departments material is excessive and in others there is downtime or shortages of material. Never mind that accidents are frequent, quality or service is substandard, excessive energy is consumed, and a great deal of time is wasted. Never mind that managers and employees are frustrated and live with stress, anxiety and insecurities, knowing the management system is unsound. Problems are ignored, conflicts are avoided, and disagreements are quickly smoothed over in an effort to "cooperate" and be "team players".

An organization, like that of an unsynchronized traffic light system, is not efficient and will have productivity problems. The human, natural, and capital resources will not be fully utilized. Late deliveries, shortages of material and parts will exist, and there will be excessive downtime and overtime. The quality of the product or service will decline and reflect the quality of management.

Participative Team Management involves all individuals working together to identify and solve problems, resolve conflicts, listen to each other, and to effectively communicate to develop a synergistic effect to achieve the organization's agreed upon goals and objectives. In PTM, individuals are striving for the best possible solutions and decisions that will enhance the organization as a whole.

Avoiding Chaos

In all organizations, policies and procedures are dictated where conformity is necessary to avoid chaos. Conformance is necessary if the organization is to achieve its goals and objectives. Conflict is detrimental if it deters the achievement of these goals. Conformity is detrimental if the policies, goals and objectives are improper or unsound. Conflicts must be resolved to determine the best policies, the best goals, and the best objectives. Once this is achieved and there is a concensus, true participative teamwork becomes the natural result and is not one that has been imposed from above.

The emphasis on communications in a conforming organization is downward, from top to bottom. In PTM, emphasis is on communications in all directions, especially listening and acting on ideas and suggestions from subordinates. A product or service usually progresses through an operation horizontally, with input from all directions. Communications should follow the flow of the material, the product, or the service. In practice, very little time is permitted for supervisors to communicate with each other. The traditional approach has often been, "Just do your job and don't worry about the next guy".

In the closing meeting of a Management Skills Development Program, the participants complete a program critique. In their critiques, a majority will express that they are now able to comprehend the problems of other departments and have gained respect for their peers by getting to know them better. As a result, they are better able to communicate and work together to solve problems, eliminate barriers and resolve conflicts. Many stated that previously, they never had the opportunity to sit down with their peers to openly communicate and discuss common problems and to seek solutions.

Participative Team Management requires an openness with a sound organizational environment toward listening, critiquing, encouraging creativity and always seeking the best solution. The implementation of PTM concepts and practices leads to the development of a sound organizational culture. *Webster's New World Dictionary* defines teamwork as: "A joint action by a group of people, in which individual interests are subordinated to group unity and efficiency; coordinated efforts by all".

In PTM development programs, managers are asked to list "Key Problems" they feel are most important and if resolved, will result in improved organizational effectiveness and increased productivity. Managers always list communications as their number one, most important problem. As indicated in the chapter on communications, everyone is aware of the problem and talks about it, but the problem still exists. The existing organizational culture does not permit effective communication. Communication problems may in fact, be a symptom of a much greater problem— unsound management concepts and practices.

Leadership Styles

Participative Team Management requires that each individual identify and recognize individual leadership styles including one's own style, as well as the positive or negative impact it may have on others. Conflicts may be an indication of creative thinking. Managers in a PTM environment manage to achieve what is best for the organization as a whole; not like the Waterloo traffic lights, where each individual treats his responsibilities as a separate entity. Individuals must learn to identify the various types of management styles and be able to work with them effectively. Identification with understanding permits a dialog. Participants must be able to see themselves, recognize the need to change and become team builders. The result is a synchronized organization with a synergistic effort—all moving in the same direction, toward the same goals.

Restrictive job descriptions limit effective PTM especially at lower levels of management and at the worker level. At a plant in Japan, it used to take a die setter four hours to change a die. Today, it takes twenty minutes. The operator, assistant and die setter are not bound by restrictive job descriptions and work together as a team to change the die. Can you imagine this kind of team participation existing with our restrictive job descriptions? The overall consideration in Participative Team Management is how an individual can help his organization. The results of a team effort are to achieve superior quality and increased productivity.

Organizations in this country are achieving similar results using Participative Team Management concepts and practices. No manager works independently. There is an overlap of each manager's responsibilities to assist each other and to critique individual and group activities toward improving productivity. Work thus becomes more meaningful, with fewer frustrations and less stress to create genuine working relationships.

1. Donald A. Spartz, "Developing an Organization that Listens", *Manufacturing Engineering*, Volume 90, No. 3, March 1983, pp.93-94.

13

THE ORGANIZATIONAL CULTURE

In the past few years the term "organizational culture" has been used as a valid and descriptive term. The term will become increasingly more meaningful. The organizational culture is easy to talk about, yet difficult to identify. In a previous chapter, organizational culture was defined as the combined management styles, practices and beliefs which determine the level of activities, and the degree of motivation and creativity of the working environment.

The term organizational culture is possibly the most descriptive, all-encompassing term developed in the field of management. Most managers readily agree that based on this definition, there are both sound and unsound organizational cultures with many somewhere in between. The manager's task is to objectively identify their current organizational culture and set in motion the management actions necessary to revitalize management practices and develop a sound organizational culture. This is no easy task. To acknowledge the possibility that one is not managing in a sound manner is difficult. To be objective in critiquing and assessing oneself is difficult if not impossible. There is a high degree of self-deception in most self-assessment.

Self-Deception

Blake and Mouton provide a statement on self-deception in their book *The New Managerial Grid*: "One indicator is that forty-five percent of managers change their self-descriptions when they compare the way they see themselves after completing a one-week Managerial Grid Seminar with how they saw themselves beforehand".[1] According to Blake and Mouton, managers have a self-deception level of 65% or higher.

The high level of self-deception provides an explanation why many training and development programs fail. Many supervisors and managers know the right answers, are aware of proper and sound management practices, and can readily pinpoint them both verbally and in writing during a development program. Many, in fact, feel they are managing soundly while their actual practices are quite different.

The manager's challenge is to objectively lead the organization on a self-identification, self-discovery experience so managers will honestly self-critique and freely change their beliefs and actions.

Whether an organizational culture is sound or unsound can be identified in day-to-day activities. The signs are the result of the management and leadership styles of the management team, especially that of the CEO and senior executives. The organizational culture is determined by leadership and management styles which have an impact and result in people reacting and responding with corresponding types of behavior.

Black, White and Gray

It would be naive to suggest that the organizational culture as reflected in behavior is either purely sound or unsound. At the same time it is nonproductive to say there is a large gray area between a sound and unsound culture; therefore, the criteria is not applicable. This is an excuse for doing nothing. If a management practice or activity is not 100% sound, then the unsound element should be identified and challenged. Self-assessment of the culture requires objectivity and candid open critiquing with a desire to excel. To ignore an unsound activity is self-deceiving.

It is safe and easy to continue the status quo and not implement any new imaginative ideas. Progressive and effective management practices breed progress, growth and excellence with high productivity. Ineffective, unsound management practices seemingly result in widening the organizational cultural gap in justifying the status quo.

In the chapter on *"Standards of Performance"*, we indicated that it is possible to identify an individual's performance gap, that being the difference between responsibilities and results. The organizational cultural gap can also be identified by measuring the difference between a sound organizational culture and an unsound organizational culture.

There are a number of organizational activities which permit a manager to make an objective assessment. Some of these activities are outlined in the following Organizational Culture Self-Assessment Profile.

ORGANIZATIONAL CULTURE
SELF-ASSESSMENT PROFILE

UNSOUND

SOUND

1. ___ Poor communications with the emphasis on downward communications.

1. ___ Communications are open and candid, individuals are receptive to new ideas and the best procedure.

2. ___ Directives and orders are given in an authoritarian manner without previous participation and are expected to be carried out without question.

2. ___ There are definite team management concepts and practices where the decision makers seek and obtain the best solutions and the most productive activities, even if it is not their own.

3. ___ There is a lack of trust between individuals. Individuals are suspicious of the motive behind actions taken, directions, policies, suggestions and communications.

3. ___ Mutual trust and respect is evident. Employees ask, suggest, confide and feel free to challenge and evaluate. Knowing that the bottom line of their efforts is that their subject(s) of discussion will be digested, evaluated and implemented with appropriate recognition if the situation warrants it.

4. ___ A sense of insecurity with barriers causing a reluctance to suggest or fully report for fear of the response. The individual perceives his superiors as not being receptive to suggestions and change. No one listens.

4. ___ Each individual feels secure based on self-confidence and mutual respect. Employees practice good listening habits and are treated fairly. They also know what is positively delegated with mutual trust.

5. ___ There is a strong emphasis on work rule enforcement and disciplinary action procedures.

5. ___ Employees self-manage and police themselves through commitment, involvement and group peer pressure. Work rules are minimal with disciplinary action seldom necessary. They appreciate management's empathy and treatment as participating human beings.

6. ___ There is a lack of goals. Top management may have goals but they have not communicated them throughout the organization.

7. ___ With the lack of goals providing individual and group direction of activities, an excessive number of employees is required to meet production requirements.

8. ___ There are no goals, objectives or Standards of Performance; therefore, time is poorly managed and is not recognized as an important resource.

9. ___ Workers, supervisors and middle managers put in their eight hours and at the sound of the whistle or when the clock strikes four, all leave regardless.

10. ___ Supervisors and managers are unaware of their management style and/or are unconcerned about the impact they have on others.

11. ___ Status quo or the present trend is accepted as good enough. We made a profit last year, don't question or suggest we change and do differently.

12. ___ Employees are working within restrictive job descriptions, concerned only about oneself vs. the group.

6. ___ Goals are established in writing, agreed on, and are measurable throughout the organization through first level supervision. Also, they are consistently updated and reviewed quarterly.

7. ___ The lean organization manages by goals with group and team efforts designed to improve productivity.

8. ___ Time is considered a resource to be used effectively in achieving goals, objectives, and Standards of Performance.

9. ___ Output per manhour is important. Individuals will put in extra energy and time to achieve agreed upon goals or handle a crisis.

10. ___ Supervisors and managers have identified their management style and are aware of the positive/negative impact it has on others.

11. ___ Status quo is not good enough. What are our opportunities, are we properly managing for change, utilizing our capital, natural and human resources to our best advantage? What we did yesterday isn't necessarily good enough today.

12. ___ Job descriptions are nonexistent. Employees work against goals, Standards of Performance and objectives.

13. ___ Delegation is poorly handled and is not considered as a means of developing people and an organization.

14. ___ Favoritism and discrimination is suggested with the practices being justified as a means to "get the job done".

15. ___ Conflicts are avoided or suppressed resulting in frustrations and anxieties.

16. ___ Problems are avoided or concealed from superiors.

17. ___ Employees are put down and suppressed.

18. ___ Decisions and practices are from above, there is no opportunity to critique performance.

19. ___ The tendency is to concentrate on what the employee is doing wrong and berate him in front of others.

20. ___ Performance is seldom or infrequently evaluated.

13. ___ Delegation is used to develop people and the organization to permit experienced workers to concentrate on the vital few activities which make the difference.

14. ___ All employees are treated in a fair and consistent manner. Employees are given an opportunity to grow by continuously learning new skills.

15. ___ Conflicts are confronted, discussed, resolved and used as opportunities and learning experiences.

16. ___ Problems are solved and are considered opportunities for improving productivity. A monthly (quarterly) summary and solutions are communicated to all employees.

17. ___ Creativity is encouraged by seeking change and new ideas with time allocated for creativity, research and development.

18. ___ There is a practice of concurrent critiquing of performance activities and decisions, always toward seeking excellence.

19. ___ Employees are recognized for contributions through positive reinforcement techniques.

20. ___ Poor performance is immediately identified with action taken to help the employee improve performance through additional training and coaching.

| 21. __ Employees have little or no input into their jobs. Their procedures are established without participation from others. | 21. __ Worker-Supervision Productivity and Development Activities are in existence and are allowed the freedom and time for self-management, identifying and solving productivity problems, and setting goals and standards. |

The task of developing a sound organizational culture is a job for every manager. It requires a sound, planned organized approach. Anything less is asking for disaster.

The Changing Environment

Changing an organizational culture means changing beliefs, attitudes and some basic assumptions on what constitutes sound management practices. This requires an openness in communications with the freedom to say what one thinks. It requires the skill of identifying the management style of managers and the patience to listen. With the understanding of beliefs which may be different from our own, an exchange can take place on an acceptable adversarial basis or better still, on a nonadversarial basis. To state that all relationships must be on a nonadversarial basis is naive. Adversarial relationships are acceptable when two sides or opinions must be presented if the best decision is to be made. A defense and a plaintiff attorney are in the courtroom on an adversarial basis. However, they conduct themselves in a professional manner, with understanding and respect for each other's responsibilities and motives. Both have a desire for the Judge to reach the best and most correct decision.

Managers can also conduct themselves in a professional manner by presenting their beliefs, ideas, opinions and suggestions on a logical, factual basis, with respect for others as equals and as human beings. Participative Team Management concepts in developing a sound organizational culture means communications are open and everyone can speak freely. Anything less is a compromise. Open communications means the decision maker has all the inputs and is able to make sound decisions which will also be the best decisions. When this is accomplished, all participants will win.

1. Robert R. Blake and Jane S. Mouton, *The New Managerial Grid* (Houston, Texas: Gulf Publishing Company, 1978), p. 1.

14

REVITALIZATION GOALS

The initial step in revitalizing the management system is understanding the organizational culture. Once this is honestly assessed, revitalization goals can be established. Objectivity is essential yet difficult, due to the high percentage of self-deception in all of us. It is also difficult because it involves change.

There are some basic requirements if goals are to be achieved. First, the goals must be in writing; second, they must be measurable, and third, there must be a set completion date for accomplishing these goals. Finally, there must be total agreement and a commitment by all involved.

Once a goal is properly established, a plan can be outlined on how the goal will be achieved. A goal will always precede the plan. The plan will restate the goal, the procedures and necessary resources to be used, who will be responsible, how progress will be measured, and a completion date to achieve the goal.

The goals reflect the present organizational cultural status and the changes which must take place. These goals must be specific, will be different in each organization, and will change as management is revitalized and a sound organizational culture is developed.

The First Step

The first step toward revitalizing the management system is to objectively assess and profile the organizational culture. This will identify weaknesses and areas where goals are needed.

A manager should be constantly alert for short-term crisis brushfire management practices. He must be aware of the end of the month rush, delays in promised deliveries, excessive downtime and undue overtime, to name only a few. Brushfire management practices are symptoms of more serious problems which need to be identified and corrected. Objective assessment and profiling of the organizational culture will provide the opportunity and identify the necessity for change and permit long-term planning.

The Second Step

The second step a manager must take is to consider all the organizational activities and develop a phased program as outlined in the chapter entitled *"Creating an Environment for Change"*. Productivity is increased by all management units working together through Participative Team Management concepts and practices.

A manager, after reading this book, should now be able to establish some very specific goals. Some examples of suggested goals, certainly not applicable to all organizations, are as follows:

1. Identify effective and noneffective management styles and their impact on the organization.
2. Develop Participative Team Management concepts and practices designed to obtain a sound organizational culture.
3. Ensure that corporate, plant and departmental goals and/or objectives are in writing and communicated to all employees.
4. Review the organizational structure to eliminate unnecessary layers of management and nonessential staff personnel.
5. Identify and assess developmental possibilities of incompetent, obsolete and surplus personnel.
6. Develop a true open door policy by receptively communicating and speaking to all people. Attempt to communicate if only to set an appointment or redirect a person to someone who can offer them assistance. The CEO, managers, and supervisors must start communicating directly and humanistically to all levels, including the workers. Communications must be approached from the standpoint of listening, motivating and taking action through proper channels, and is not be be used as a devise to usurp responsibilities.
7. Establish a Standards of Performance program with first level management, clerical and staff personnel.
8. Establish a Management by Objectives program for middle and upper management.
9. Evaluate each manager's responsibilities and activities to identify areas where delegation will create growth through the development of new skills and increased productivity.
10. Identify barriers to effective communications. Concentrate on

having managers develop good listening skills, with the ability to express true empathy and provide timely feedback.

11. Develop staff attitudes and practices that will positively reinforce their job positions and result in their providing greater assistance and support to line personnel to increase productivity.

12. Establish a pilot worker/supervisor productivity improvement program to gradually include all employees when a sound organizational culture has been developed. This program should be a normal part of every supervisor-manager's job.

13. Develop a worker self-management attitude with discipline being de-emphasized, and a flex-time policy with emphasis on group-developed standards and results achieved.

14. Eliminate restrictive job descriptions and develop worker trust and loyalty based on self-management, using established standards with recognition for performance.

Established organizational goals provide the direction and the plan outlines how the goals will be achieved.

15

SUMMARY

The need to improve management effectiveness is apparent. Productivity for many organizations has been declining as a result of ineffective management. The action taken to correct this trend has often involved short-term planning and shortsighted management practices with superficial treatment of the symptoms. The cause of declining productivity rests with management systems which have fostered an organizational culture which is not sound.

Revitalization and development requires long-term goals and planning with a very systematic, organized approach toward the process of change. Development of sound leadership which is receptive and seeking change with the ability to set high organizational and development objectives is essential to management's revival.

These objectives should be to:

1. Seek and obtain organizational excellence.
2. Seek and obtain high quality service and products.
3. Eliminate nonproductive workers and nonproductive activities.
4. Develop a quality participative team relationship throughout the organization.

Redirection

CEO's and top managers are in a position to identify shortsighted activities, emphasize long-range planning, and leave short-term planning to the front-line level of supervision. There is a need to move from treating the symptoms to dealing effectively with the causes by way of identifying the reasons why organizations have productivity problems. This means there is a need for some "demanagement" training to erase learned management habits and practices that are not justifiable, productive and effective. The ineffective manager must be redirected to develop effective leadership skills and

Participative Team Management concepts and practices. This is where an internal Development Center will become a trend in the near future.

Natural progression will move organizations toward Participative Team Management concepts and practices if they are to remain competitors in today's marketplace. This trend will be resisted by some and will be at the very minimum, difficult for the traditional manager. Companies that take comfort in continuing to operate under their well-established, traditional guidelines, may also stand firm against this trend of the '80s—to their own detriment.

Eli Whitney achieved success by designing both a product and a production line as one system. This same thought must be a foremost objective as managers involved in the transformation process agree that developing and acquiring Participative Team Management concepts and practices is a complex, long-term process. There are no simple or magic formulas. The process of change requires sound leadership with the ability to objectively assess the present organizational culture and establish appropriate goals. Communications must be open with workers feeling free to express their feelings and voice their opinions. Listening skills will improve in the process when workers are recognized as equals and as contributing human beings, and are treated accordingly. It will become more easy to identify and correct problems and to confront and resolve conflicts.

The practice of managing by getting things done through others at all cost, will have to be reconsidered. Managers need to concentrate on developing people to perform their necessary work effectively, and at the same time enjoy themselves. Organizations will have to establish internal Developmental Centers to accomplish this. The first priority will be the development of people, quality and service. This can not be accomplished by directives. It will be accomplished by managers who can develop the goals and initiate a development plan with the patience to direct its implementation and see it through to completion.

In writing we have deliberately left out theory. It was our intention to stick with the basics because we believe that is where the answers lie. We have included case studies because we believe they provide a beginning to stimulate action. The use of actual in-company problems and case studies in the development process are more effective than theorizing. In addition, resolving in-company problems in the developmental process results in an immediate improvement in productivity. In recommending the basics, we suggest avoiding the elaborate, self-serving administrative staff programs that have been in style in the past.

The process of revitalizing management and developing a sound organizational culture is based on valid principles applied through an organized, systematic process. We encourage the reader to question, challenge and develop individual personal beliefs. Self-examination is a very difficult and frightening undertaking. It is, after all, our personal beliefs which determine our behavior and the results we achieve.

With self-preservation being the first law of nature, the inclination to maintain a comfort zone through consistent, familiar behavior, is a trait that becomes common to all mankind. If this tendency directs us toward practices which limit our resources, we may do well to remember the words of Thomas Jefferson when he said:

"I know no safe depository of the ultimate powers of the society but the people themselves; and if we think them not enlightened enough to exercise their control with a wholesome discretion, the remedy is not to take it from them, but to inform their discretion."

APPENDIX

Developmental Case Studies

Developmental Case Studies are listed to stimulate discussion and analysis. Case Studies are skill development tools to be used in obtaining participation and determining the contributing causes of problems. Case Studies may be used as learning experiences, and to establish a course of action. Case Studies should be viewed as a starting point. Actual internal problems and conflicts should then be incorporated into a similar study. In-house Case Studies should be developed in a manner that will not embarrass anyone within the organization.

CASE STUDY 1
MANAGEMENT PERSPECTIVES

The S.Z. Manufacturing Company designs and builds machines for industry. The bargaining unit is organized, is on piecework with wages being comparable with others in their industry, but better than average for their geographical location. The majority of their plant employees are considered skilled. S.Z. is a division of a conglomerate which launched a productivity improvement program 12 months ago. S.Z. has been profitable, although the profit margin has been gradually declining. Sales volume continues to increase annually, partially due to price increases and increases in the number of units manufactured. The size and complexity of S.Z's machines has been increasing due to customer requirements. The quality of the product has

143

remained stable. In the past year, competitors' products, selling at a comparable price, have improved significantly in performance, appearance and quality. Foreign competition is starting to move into the market.

The Corporate Productivity Improvement Program was based on sales volume, units produced and profits. Each division manager was to develop and implement a plan. The S.Z. manager based his program on sales.

The S.Z. manager has called a meeting of the Controller, and the manager's of the Sales, Quality Control, Manufacturing and Engineering Departments to identify the reasons for the poor profit performance and to establish a productivity improvement program for the new year.

The Sales Manager complains about late deliveries, poor quality and field complaints regarding product performance.

The Controller reports on increased material cost, high utility cost, increased overtime, an increase in the number of production workers, rework costs, and high in-process and finished inventories.

The Quality Control Manager reports rejects and rework are up due to poor attitudes. "People just don't take pride in their work" he claims. In addition, his department cannot inspect every part. Parts are ready for assembly and are found to be machined improperly.

The Manufacturing Manager feels Personnel is not hiring good people. His supervisors aren't trained and they are too busy to take time for training. He requires them to be on the floor 95% of their time. His department's output was increased and met the improvement plan. The Controller points out that the increased cost of labor exceeded output. The Manufacturing Manager, complains that the engineering drawings are not current.

The Engineering Manager reports they are doing the best they can with the manpower available. In addition, he is required to send his engineers into the field to troubleshoot problems caused by manufacturing mistakes.

Action
1. How should the manager of S.Z. Manufacturing proceed.
2. Define "Productivity".
3. Where does the problem lie in S.Z.?
4. How should S.Z. be measuring productivity?
5. Develop the Productivity Improvement Goals and Plan for S.Z.
6. What controls should the manager put in place?

CASE STUDY 2
SUBSTANDARD PERFORMANCE

Joe is a clerk responsible for receiving and inspecting incoming material. He checks the material against a purchase order and routes the material to the respective departments. Joe has been on the job for six years and has always worked for Frank, his immediate supervisor.

Joe gets along well with everyone, is cooperative, has a good attendance record and no known personal problems. His Personnel file is clean. He has received regular annual pay increases and is due to be promoted to Senior Receiving Clerk because of seniority.

Joe's actual job performance has never been good. He makes an average of six mistakes a week. Frank has been aware of the mistakes. Frank has determined that these mistakes cost the company about $800 a week in receiving poor material, cost of rerouting to proper departments, and production downtime due to material shortages. The Production Superintendnent wants Joe fired now.

Action
1. Define the problem.
2. What is Joe's problem? Is Joe the real problem?
3. What action should Frank take?
4. How can a problem like this be identified and prevented in the future?
5. Should Joe—or will Joe, because of his seniority—be promoted?

NOTE: This case works well in role playing—for the individual playing Joe's part, add the factor that he has poor eyesight and does not want anyone to know it.

CASE STUDY 3
PRINCIPLES OF DEVELOPMENT

The S.J. Lesco Manufacturing Company, a publicly held firm, has been in business for 60 years. The primary products are compressors. Their business has grown the same as their industry and generally follows the economic cycles. In an economic upture, Lesco hires and in a downturn, Lesco lays off in accord with the union contract. When recalling those on layoff, the company has found a pattern where above average workers are not available because they have found other work. As a result, the company has a mature, steady, older, conforming group of employees.

Lesco's CEO has recognized this situation and has suggested a worker-management development program. The CEO is looking for suggestions and input from his key executives. So far, each executive has had a different priority. As a consequence, nothing is happening. He considers his key executives to be Ken the Controller; John the Engineering Manager; Joe, Sales and Marketing Manager; Paul, Manufacturing Manager; Russ, Quality Control Manager, and Julia the Manager of Human Resources.

These executives are described as follows:

Ken the Controller is busy and has found it safer not to take a position until there is a majority opinion. Then he goes with the majority. He sees their net profit slightly up, but he recognizes a need for a facility expansion including robotics and a state of the art computer system.

John, the Engineering Manager is young, was aggressive, but has been restrained by the Manufacturing Manager even though he does not report to him. John is now reluctant to speak up, although he agrees with the Controller that expansion and robotics are needed. He is not convinced that a new computer system is necessary at this time.

Joe, Sales and Marketing Manager, wants more advertising dollars and is operating with a goal of increasing sales by 10% over the last year. He is rarely in town to attend a meeting. Joe's sales goal for the last year was 10%; however, sales were actually down due to the economy. He is receiving more customer complaints on product failures. Failed units are automatically replaced if failure occurs within one year after purchase.

Paul, Manufacturing Manager, says Joe stays out of town so that he does not have to get involved. He blames Joe for their high inventories due to the sales force. He believes in internal development, however, due to the economy, he considers it a luxury which is not affordable at this time. He wants robots to replace the lazy workers. He is willing to send a few middle managers to an outside seminar to become current with their state of the art in manufacturing. Generally, he feels he should continue on-the-job training and development of people through trial and error.

Russ, the Quality Control Manager, has no problems. He believes rejects are low and parts and compressors are being built per engineering specifications.

Julia, Human Resource Manager, believes in training and management development. She has been on the job for five years. Julia spends most of her time in meetings and dealing with grievances and EEOC problems. She has recommended the company purchase an off-the-shelf canned training program. It is inexpensive and participants could partially complete the program on their own time.

Action

1. Develop a strategic CEO plan for total development of the organization.
2. Identify the key problems in terms of organizational practices.
3. How can each manager deal with the other managers and obtain Participative Team Management decisions?

CASE STUDY 4
CREATING AN ENVIRONMENT FOR CHANGE

Kevin Jackson, President of the Douglas Department Store chain has decided to improve the corporate image and responsiveness to quality and service to the customer. He has decided to start with the corporate staff. There are presently 296 people employed in the corporate office, which he feels is much too large. He has instructed his secretary, Kim, to send out a Memo asking for ideas to present to the meetings. The responses amounted to justification for status quo and entrenchment. Jackson realizes he has probably contributed to these problems by emphasizing short-term performance.

Jackson wants to open up communications, encourage creativity, and is willing to risk changing from short-term to long-term planning. This means changing the organizational culture. In the past, he tried MBO and it failed. He has suggested incorporating the Standards of Performance; however, the managers feel their jobs cannot be objectively measured.

Action
1. Develop a strategic development plan and a schedule to meet Kevin Jackson's needs.

CASE STUDY 5
SUPERVISION

Hank Bates, Plant Manager of A.D. Electronics Company, is in the process of selecting two new first line supervisors. The openings have occurred in the Assembly Department due to a surge of orders. A second shift is to be added in two weeks.

The present supervisory personnel are longtime senior employees. They work well together, cooperate, and have a minimum of problems. They are treated fairly, with each usually receiving the same percentage pay increase each year. Bates wants the new supervisors to fit in and get along with everyone.

Bates is relying on his Superintendent, Clarence Lee, to nominate the new supervisors for his approval. Clarence selected two individuals with good records, each having several years of seniority in the bargaining unit. Clarence obtained the Personnel Manager's approval on both individuals. Bates also approved and offered each a promotion into supervision. Both rejected the promotions stating they would lose their seniority by going into supervision, and with their present pay incentives, would be making about the same salary. In addition, both expressed the belief that the present first line supervisors spend all of their time expediting parts and doing paper work.

Bates doesn't believe the Superintendent and Personnel Manager should consider further internal promotions, due to their attitudes toward supervision. Bates decides to solve the problem by hiring individuals from the outside for the two supervisory positions.

Action
1. Discuss how Bates handled the internal selection.
2. What mistakes in assumptions and actions did Bates make?
3. Is there a problem with the way the company is managed? If so, what?
4. Is Bates solving the problem by hiring from the outside?
5. Establish an internal revitalization program for Bates.

CASE STUDY 6
SUPERVISION

Harry has been an employee with the company for 10 years. His present classification is a power press operator. His performance has gradually slipped over the past six months; however, it is still average and considered to be acceptable. His Personnel file reflects good performance.

While Denise Munroe, his supervisor, is talking with him on a specification for a new part, she detects a strong odor of beer. Harry's speech is slightly slurred and his eyes are blurry. He has been on the job (second shift) for two hours and has not left his work station. Munroe notices his work is not up to standard. In addition, she feels it is unsafe to let him continue operating his press. Munroe is convinced she must take some action. She considers firing, however, the last time she fired someone, the Personnel Department reinstated the employee with back pay and with no explanation to her as to their decision.

Munroe considers letting Harry rest in her office or sending him to First-Aid to let the nurse decide, but remembers that the second shift works without a nurse on duty. She then considers sending him to First-Aid to "sleep it off". Munroe finally decides to confront Harry with his problem and sends him home in a cab. Initially, Harry angrily objects, but then agrees to leave peacefully as long as he is will be paid for the full shift.

Action
1. Were Munroe's actions appropriate?
2. Is there an underlying problem within the organization?
3. From a sound management practice, what is needed?

CASE STUDY 7
DELEGATION

John Smith has just been hired as the president of a major *Fortune* "500" company. In his first visit to a west coast plant, Smith decides to take a casual tour of the operation with Wayne, the Plant Manager. Smith believes in spending time in the plant, observing and listening.

Smith and Wayne spend most of the day in the plant. Returning to Wayne's office, Smith makes a few notes and then starts outlining his observations:

(a) Very few of the employees knew who Wayne was and were surprised to see him in the plant. Wayne's response is that he is too busy and he delegates responsibility through the management hierarchy.

(b) Smith noted several first line supervisors doing employees work while the employees sat and watched. One supervisor was sweeping the floor as they entered his department.

(c) Some employees were working hard, while others had slack time. Wayne indicated that they each work uniformly within their job descriptions.

(d) Several employees questioned why the company did certain things and offered suggested improvements in the use of equipment and in procedures.

(e) Smith noted obvious quality, scheduling and inventory problems, all of which seemed to be accepted as routine. Wayne mentions that he always meets production and profit goals.

Action
1. Define the problems and their causes.
2. How should Smith, the president, handle the situation?

CASE STUDY 8
MEASURING INDIVIDUAL PRODUCTIVITY

The Standards of Performance have been in effect for all first level supervision and support personnel. The Standards of Performance were developed by the Human Resource Department. Each participant felt that for the first time, their on-the-job performance would determine their merit increase.

In the first year, some of the participants exceeded their Standards of Performance. Others fell short of achieving an acceptable level of performance, a fact which the Plant Superintendent continuously reminded them of in weekly production staff meetings.

In a salary review meeting, there is total disagreement between the Human Resource Manager, the Plant Superintendent, the Plant Manager and the Office Manager. The Human Resource Manager has reverted back to talking about Job Descriptions and a structured salary plan. The Plant Superintendent and Plant Manager want to do as in the past—give everyone an 8% increase so all will be happy. The Office Manager likes the Standards of Performance but does not have the time to meet with each employee and evaluate their results vs. their standards. The Controller doesn't care as long as the expense budget is not exceeded. However, he firmly believes that they should take the time for a performance evaluation based on the Standards of Performance, and each individual should be given merit increases based on performance. The General Manager wants everyone to agree and tells them to meet and decide.

Action
1. What went wrong with the program?
2. Should they ignore the Standards of Performance? What effect will it have on the organization?
3. Why are there objections to the Standards of Performance?
4. Can or should the Standards of Performance be saved and used effectively to measure individual performance?
5. What are the underlying management problems?

CASE STUDY 9
COMMUNICATIONS

The ZE Manufacturing Company designs, fabricates, and sells leisure lawn furniture. It is a privately held organization.

Paul has been the plant manager of the fabricating and assembly division for five years. Paul encourages competition between the two shift superintendents based on units of output. This competition has resulted in some conflicts between the two superintendents. Frequently, one complains that the other takes the best orders and leaves problems for the next shift, which causes shift start-up delays. On occasion, each has accused the other of sabotage; however, this was humorously accepted as part of the game.

Paul holds a production meeting every Monday morning. In this meeting he sets the schedule for the week. In the past, he has discovered that when meeting only with the two superintendents, very little is communicated down to the first level of supervision. As a result, he decided one year ago to include key front line supervisors in the weekly production meetings.

Paul now feels he has the following problems:

(a) Production, Quality, and Scrap Control have not improved.
(b) Confidential discussions seem to leak out at the same rate as over the past five years.
(c) Paul cannot understand why, when he gives specific instructions to a front line supervisor in the staff meetings, his instructions are never properly carried out. In questioning the group whether they understood his instructions, all say they did and can repeat them verbatim, except the individual to whom the instructions were directed. This has caused Paul to lose his temper and state that if they cannot follow simple instructions, he will get someone who can.
(d) After Paul's outburst, the meetings ran smoothly with a minimum of discussion.
(e) Scheduling conflicts between departments have been increasing.

Action

(1) Is Paul seeing the symptoms or the problems?
(2) What are the real problems?
(3) How can Paul correct the situation?
(4) Outline the steps in developing effective, open communications.

CASE STUDY 10
MOTIVATION

An efficiency expert reports to the Plant Manager that the production workers are operating at 55% efficiency. The expert feels, and the Controller agrees, that a break-even point is 65% based on present costs and prices. The expert's analysis indicates the problem is peer pressure to maintain a slow and steady pace. Something has to be done to motivate the workers to work harder, smarter and faster. He indicates there are potentially outstanding performer's who are being pressured to not out perform the average and substandard workers. Everyone cooperates, there are no serious problems or conflicts. The supervisors spend their time completing paper work, expediting material, in meetings and handling grievances, activities which are considered a nuisance.

In a meeting with management, the efficiency expert recommends an incentive program based on piecework standards. The supervisors report their hands are tied due to the union contract and a lack of upper management support.

The Plant Superintendent doesn't think the efficiency expert understands the problem. All he needs is the backing to set a few examples and fire a few of the troublemakers.

The Purchasing Manager says he can buy an incentive and motivational promotion program. He feels such a program will inspire the workers to be more productive.

The Personnel Manager suggests an employee contest where high performance is eligible for a drawing of prizes.

Action
1. What is the problem(s)?
2. What should the Plant Manager do?
3. Develop a detailed Developmental and Productivity Plan.

CASE STUDY 11
PRODUCT MARKET WORTHINESS

A Manufacturing Manager, J.D. Stevens, is receiving an increase in the number of complaints on the quality of the products, household appliances. These complaints have been coming from the Customer Service Department, Quality Control, Sales, and the Legal Department. The president has asked him to look into the problem and take care of it.

The complaints are not new—they have always been accepted as part of the job. J.D. has traditionally operated within the budget established by the Controller.

In investigating the problem he finds the following: Customer Services has been receiving more complaints; however, the increase seems to be due to a trend of a more discriminating public, with a tendency to return products that are not perfect.

The Legal Department has received complaints about an electrical switch. There are two cases of the customer receiving a minor electrical shock. According to the supplier, the switch has not undergone a design change, nor has the quality control of the product changed.

The Quality Inspection Department confirms that the in-plant reject rate has remained the same and has the figures to prove it. They have added three inspectors in the past year due to production increases.

The Sales Manager reports competition is increasing with a higher quality product at the same price. Their sales have increased slightly in each of the past five years; however, their market share is decreasing. The Sales Manager feels the only difference between their product and the competition's is in appearance, which is the Manufacturing Managers problem. The Manufacturing Manager feels sales is not doing a good job of selling.

Action

1. How should the Manufacturing Manager proceed?
2. Develop a plan for the Manufacturing Manager to present to the president of the company.

CASE STUDY 12
PARTICIPATIVE TEAM MANAGEMENT DEVELOPMENT

A medium size manufacturing firm hired Russell Thomas as the new General Manager to turn the organization around. Sales were slipping, there were quality problems, employee attitudes were poor and morale was low. He instructed his two Administrative Assistants, Jolene and Renee to look into the matter and report back to him.

Thomas immediately became familiar with and took control of the various departments. He then spent time wandering around the departments listening and observing. Two weeks later he with his two assistants jotted down the following observations:

(a) Quality is poor.

(b) Plant layout is a problem.

(c) Housekeeping is atrocious.

(d) The hourly workers are suspicious and reluctant to talk.

(e) First line supervisors range from being very talkative to noncommittal. Most were reluctant to criticize.

(f) Plant Engineering seemed to be fighting fires.

(g) Maintenance complained of constant breakdowns due to poor operators. As a result, they had to work overtime during the week and every Saturday.

(h) The Plant Superintendent was efficient, managed with authority, knew what was going on.

(i) The Engineering Manager indicated he is unable to hire and keep good engineers that know the equipment and processes. His department is short of personnel and has a high turnover.

(j) The Plant Superintendent was aware of the quality problems caused by poor workmanship. He wanted to hire more inspectors to identify the rejects.

(k) A common complaint was blaming others for the problems, with a feeling that "Management" does not care.

(l) The Personnel Department is overloaded with grievances, EEOC problems, hiring, firing, benefit programs, wage and salary administration and endless meetings.

(m)The Purchasing Department purchases what is ordered and the Accounting Department reports on the results of the organization.

Thomas calls a meeting of all department heads and outlines his observations. The department heads initially listen without comment. Thomas specifically asked the Plant Superintendent if he had missed anything. The Plant Superintendent responded that the workers don't take pride in their work and supervisors don't know how to discipline. Personnel hires people that don't want to work, Maintenance just wants overtime, Engineering doesn't know what they are doing, and the Accounting Department should spend some time in the plant. Others jumped in with accusations and justifications. Chaos developed.

Thomas announced he wanted to concentrate on Supervisory-Management Skill Development and Participative Team Management practices.

Action

1. Develop the objections to Thomas' concluding suggestions.
2. What obstacles should Thomas anticipate?
3. Who should Thomas select to coordinate and implement his suggestions?
4. How should progress be measured?
5. Develop a revitalization program for the organization.

INDEX